D L PHILLIPS

born an angel

Learning to live again

D L PHILLIPS

born an angel

Learning to live again

MEREO

Mereo Books

1A The Wool Market Dyer Street Cirencester Gloucestershire GL7 2PR
An imprint of Memoirs Publishing www.mereobooks.com

Born an Angel: 978-1-86151-899-6

First published in Great Britain in 2018
by Mereo Books, an imprint of Memoirs Publishing

The address for Memoirs Publishing Group Limited can be found
at www.memoirspublishing.com

Cover design and artwork - Ray Lipscombe

The Memoirs Publishing Group Ltd Reg. No. 7834348

Typeset in 10/16pt Century Schoolbook
by Wiltshire Associates Publisher Services Ltd.
Printed and bound in Great Britain by Biddles Books

CONTENTS

INTRODUCTION

When I started writing this book I knew that there would be some people who wouldn't – or couldn't – bring themselves to read it, but also those who, mostly through their own experience either directly or indirectly with this tragedy, would read past the introduction. After nearly three decades and my own personal experiences, I understand the acceptance, understanding and appreciation some will find from my story, and maybe even some solace in knowing they aren't alone in their pain and suffering. But then, too, there are others to whom the subject of stillbirth and the loss of a child remains taboo, too awkward to talk about, too painful, too emotional or depressing to think that this happens to real people in real life today as it did many years ago. My story starts in 1986 when I was just 16 years old. It starts here so as to give an insight into where it all began. Today, more than three decades on, I still live with the memories and the pain, silently now. It left a scar that I don't keep on show, mostly because I don't need to – I know it's always there – but over the years I've been asked, and it has been suggested, that I don't carry any kind of scar. For this I feel guilt and a sense of shame that I know I shouldn't; I have put the feeling of others, even strangers, before my own so as not to show them my scar in case it makes them uncomfortable or left feeling awkward. For this reason I want to tell my story openly; no one is forcing you to read this book, but one day I hope it will help others to come to see that, while it should never be the case that a parent survives their child, there are mothers, fathers and families who, despite the anguish and heartache, live through and survive the tragedy of losing a child.

CHAPTER 1

How we met – Sweet Sixteen

Autumn 1986, my final year at school. Lots of life choices to make: college, YTS (youth training scheme, in essence working for a pittance – it is no longer around, I wonder why?) or work? I knew I would opt for work. I wanted to earn money and be independent, travel, learn to drive – no one in my family could – get a car and have nice things. It was the era of punk and the New Romantics and I was part of the latter; bright clothes, big earrings, big shoulder pads and even bigger hairstyles, often back combed as wide as the shoulders. Everything about the '80s was big and bold.

School hadn't been too harrowing – although I was never one of the really popular girls attracting the attention of all the good looking boys, I was still invited to parties. I was in one of the higher classes – one of the smarter ones they said – although I believed I was only there because I had appeared in a TV documentary and played the main role of the author of a book about growing up in Birmingham in the 1900s. I was also an extra in a few other TV series, and the photographs Central TV had issued to the school were still on prime view in the foyer of my secondary school for everyone to see, despite the fact it had been aired a couple of years previously. I got ridiculed by some of the students, but it brought me my moment of fame and I knew it would be one for the grandkids someday, if I was lucky enough to have my own family.

I was one of five children growing up on a council estate, second eldest but the eldest daughter, the one that 'should always know better' according to my parents, although my mom knew I was somewhat of a risk taker and always said 'if anyone will do it our Debbie will'. Boy did I live up to that in the forthcoming years, partaking in charity parachute jumps for one thing.

My parents raised us well, we never got into trouble with the authorities and always did well in school, we had earned the nickname locally of 'The Waltons', due to the TV series and the fact we were always seen together. During June of 1986 my younger sister had been involved in a road traffic accident and almost lost her life. My mom had always been extremely superstitious, and the day before had been Friday 13th. Mom would always worry beyond belief and pretty much kept us under house arrest for a full day on any Friday 13th, but it was the following day whilst mom was at work that the accident happened. My sister had wanted to go shopping on the bus with her elder friend who lived around the corner; my dad knew mom wouldn't have allowed her to but he agreed to let her go – their secret. She had seen the bus coming and ran down the opposite side of the green hill in front of our house to catch the bus with her friend. It was a busy road to cross at the best of times; being a Saturday it was devoid of rush hour traffic but still busy. She had picked up speed going downhill and thought she could make it across the busy road; pedestrian traffic lights and railings had been installed but not at that time commissioned, her judgement was wrong and she collided with a car travelling too fast. It catapulted her into the newly installed railings and over them; she left one almighty dent in those railings, I recall, and they were later replaced again. It was a harrowing time for us all and my mom held us together well. My sister lost half her body blood and had to undergo a transfusion, her nose was pretty much non-existent and she had to have it rebuilt, she suffered a fractured skull, broken arm and crushed leg for which she had to undergo operations, and by the autumn of '86 she was home, lucky to be alive but in a wheelchair and receiving home tutoring.

It was early autumn and still relatively mild weather; I had gone around to one of my girlfriends' houses, and teenage girls being teenage girls we talked about the only thing there was at that age – boys. She had once dated a lad that was an identical twin and knew where he hung out. She was still quite struck by him and we decided to walk up to the park near the estate he would normally be seen around, hoping to catch a glimpse of him. I was a big Madonna fan and I recall 'True Blue' being in the charts around that time. I knew every word, not just to that Madonna song, but to every one of them; I had bought every vinyl record I could – 7" and 12" if it was available – as this meant I got to listen to the extended version of a Madonna song.

That evening we walked up to the park and stayed around the play area for a bit, but there was no sign of her lost love so although we knew it was outside our allowable area we walked over to the estate where he lived and spent most evenings after school. It was dark and starting to get a little chilly, so after no success we started to head back towards home. It was then that she spotted him at the bus stop with two friends – or so we thought. As we got closer, the friends recognised my girlfriend and we walked toward the bus stop; it turned out to be the old flame's identical twin – a slight speck in those baby blue eyes were apparently the way to tell them apart – dark wavy hair, beautiful smile and killer blue eyes. I could see why she had fallen for the brother. I was taken aback when he started talking to me and taking an interest, in me! Oh my, I was love-struck;

Cupid had aimed that arrow right at me and serendipity played a big part in that. Unfortunately for my friend, it turned out that his brother was quite serious with a very stunning girl and had been for a while, and he himself was smitten. Sad for my girlfriend that it hadn't turned out the way she had wanted, but I was walking on clouds and we arranged to meet again the following evening, at the same bus stop.

I remember going home that evening, getting my diary from its hiding place (I shared a room with my two sisters so nothing was sacred, everything had to be well hidden if you wanted any secrets or privacy) and writing all about him and doodling hearts. I hardly slept that night, wishing the hours away to the next evening.

The days together went into weeks, months, even. I would stay at his most weekends, even babysitting his younger sister while his parents went out to the local pub and he went out with friends or his brother. By this time I was working as an office junior and was graduating to a trainee book keeper; life was great and I felt I was living every girl's dream. I was a virgin when we met and after seven months we finally made love. I thought it was so romantic; we squirrelled ourselves away and hid in some bushes, it was a clear night and there were many stars in the sky. I was scared, trembling even, but he was gentle and understanding. He was my first love and I knew we would always be together; my first sexual experience had been hasty and yet loving, and to me very special, not something I felt I regretted. Life was laid out for me and I was loving every minute, so happy and yet still so naive.

In 1988 I started going ice skating with friends; I had never skated before but soon picked it up. I met some great new friends during this time, and I would skate two to three times a week, mostly at weekends with my girlfriends. There was a very handsome lad that all the girls swooned after, he was an amazing skater and heartbreakingly gorgeous with striking Italian looks; we called him the Rock. We became friends and eventually it began to turn to more; I felt so guilty, but my boyfriend had been spending more time going out with his friends and I had been spending more weekends alone at his parents' house babysitting his younger sister. The attention I was getting from the Rock eventually swayed me and I ended my relationship and began dating him. I remember getting off the bus one Sunday afternoon and my 'now ex' was sitting on the hill in front of my house. He was sobbing and walked over to me absolutely furious – he had discovered I had met someone else and that this was the reason for my ending things. He was devastated – and seeing him, so was I. Eventually, a couple of weeks later, I said goodbye to the Rock and we decided to give things another go and try to be more attentive to one another. I remember thinking about whether I had made the right decision; I was still so young, but soon after we fell back into the relationship with ease and I realised at that moment that I really was with my first love, and thought he was my forever love.

In 1989, Batman and Lethal Weapon 2 were hot at the movies, and the hit TV show Dynasty came to an end after nine series of the Colbys and Carringtons, with the final episode leaving viewers with cliff-hangers that would never be resolved – I was devastated. That year we went on our first holiday together to Jersey in the Channel Isles, visiting the tartan bar, St Helier and beautiful cove beaches. His parents were there at the same time but staying in a different part of the island, and we occasionally met up with them and his little sister during our week there. I remember falling asleep sunbathing on the beach and waking up thirsty. I had a can of pop at the side of me over which I had placed the heel of my shoe in an attempt to keep anything from getting into to the open top. I picked up the can and took a swig of pop; it was then that I felt something in my mouth and spat it out quickly – the shoe idea hadn't worked, and a wasp had found its way under and into the can. Fortunately I wasn't stung and the holiday continued to be wonderful and without any further dramas, but already having a fear of wasps it was a hard lesson learned, and since that day I have never drunk from an open can or bottle after it has been left for a while.

We often went on nights out together; he was a great dancer and all the girls loved him. I was young and quite often felt insecure, even more so because of all the attention he gained and seemed to crave, but we did have fun. We had arguments too, sometimes quite rowdy ones; I remember once getting into an argument in a pub over some girl flirting and he hit me – first and last time! I hit him back; unfortunately for me, I only took one swing but he ducked, I hit a brick fireplace and ended up at the hospital. I had chipped a bone in my knuckle, nothing too serious but very painful, however there was never a fist raised again by either of us. We seemed to just grow together organically and despite the usual young love tiffs, we stayed together and let the path lead us where it may.

It was March 1990 when we discovered we were pregnant. We had talked about having children and a house and all the things dreams seem to be made of when you don't know any better and about the difficulties and responsibilities of raising a family and paying your own bills, but it wasn't meant to have been just yet. Nonetheless, we were both overjoyed. Telling our parents was our biggest fear. I had got on well with his parents but mine hadn't approved of him much; he couldn't hold a job down for long and my dad especially took a dislike to him from the start when he had said he wasn't interested in football back in the early days of our relationship. Things between him and my dad never did improve; I think my dad knew right from the start it wouldn't end well. My family were big football fans and followers, all supporting the local team with the exception of my mom who avidly supported Liverpool for many, many years and still does to this day. She continues to defend her team vehemently; I myself always thought it had something more to do with the '60s and the Beatles, and not so much to do with football.

My mom had fought my corner and that of my siblings unconditionally and with purpose, my relationship during the latter part of the '80s being the root of many disagreements between my parents. I remember at one point seeing my dad with a nasty cut on his nose; Mom later told me they had argued over his ignorance and attitude towards my boyfriend on one of the very rare occasions when he had stayed at my parents'. The disagreement had got a little heated and Mom had thrown an ashtray at my dad which, to her surprise, had landed perfectly at the bridge of my dad's nose leaving him with a scar as a permanent reminder.

We finally plucked up the courage to tell our parents about the baby a few days after we had found out ourselves. Neither set of parents was too pleased; we had all the lectures about only being 19 and having our whole lives ahead of us, and about not both having steady jobs and savings behind us. Neither of us could at that point drive either; I had been taking lessons but stupidly put them on hold when I found out about the pregnancy as I felt the money for lessons would be better spent on items we would need for our baby. We were in love and having a baby, we didn't care and were naïve to the future stresses and strains; we were so happy and started making plans for our future together. We had no idea how we would manage when I went on maternity leave, as he hadn't managed to hold down a proper job for any length of time since leaving school almost four years previously, but we didn't worry, we would manage somehow. Soon after we had broken the news, he proposed to me and I was over the moon. He had got me the most beautiful cluster engagement ring (which I now suspect was purchased from money I had lent him, so it's quite possible I had bought it myself as he never repaid me when he borrowed money). However, the news of the pregnancy didn't bode well at all with one parent, my dad. It only proved to strain our relationship further over the coming months.

CHAPTER 2

The pregnancy – me and bump

At 12 weeks I had my first scan. We were so excited, both mothers – grandmothers-to-be – came with us. It was the most precious and amazing moment, seeing the little figure in black and white on the screen and hearing a little heart beat felt surreal. Suddenly the reality of being parents was there right in front of our eyes, we had created this tiny little person and I knew I loved every little finger and toe right there and then. Suddenly my life was about another person, our child, made from our love, and we couldn't wait to meet our little one. We got pictures of the scan, not as good and clear as they are today, but back then who cared – it looked like a blob on a piece of paper, difficult for anyone but me to make out, but I knew that what I was seeing was my child. Their arms would be the most precious thing I would ever wear around my neck and I felt whole, scared and unaware of what to expect, but totally in love with the black and white blob on the picture I was holding. How could anything be greater than this moment? My due date was the end of November, so we would have our first Christmas together with our precious little one. Christmas had always been my favourite time of the year and this year was going to be extra special; we were going to be a family!

It was after that first scan that we decided to make plans to be married before our baby was born. It was going to be a shotgun wedding, we knew, and people would talk, but it was also because his mother was Catholic and wanted us to have a proper ceremony and not a registry office. This would be a challenge given that the pregnancy would soon begin to show. My soon to be mother-in-law had recently lost her only surviving parent and had received some inheritance, and she said she was prepared to help with the cost of the wedding. She and I had always been close and spent a lot of time together chatting and going on shopping outings; when she first received her inheritance I remember her asking me to go to an exclusive boutique with her to buy an outfit as she had never been able to afford such quality clothing and wanted to treat herself. She intended to buy an exquisite outfit, one that she could also wear for the wedding. We spent hours in the boutique and finally found the perfect two piece; she looked amazing, a million dollars, and we came out of there full of plans and hopes for the future.

The following week, his mother and I visited a church local to where they lived and I often stayed. The whole experience terrified me – I was going to give myself to someone for life. Later that day we sat and discussed the matter, all three of us, and made a second appointment at the church for just the two of us to attend, to make arrangements and set a date for our wedding. It needed to be soon or there was a chance the clergyman would notice the pregnancy and refuse to marry us; also I may have had difficulty in finding a dress to fit and hide the growing bump in my tummy. Like all girls I wanted the big dress, the big moment, but I knew it would be somewhat of a compromise given the circumstances.

Unfortunately as the day arrived for our meeting at the church, he didn't show. I was devastated. When he finally showed up he claimed to have forgotten and said he would rearrange the appointment. It never happened; maybe a lucky escape … .

The pregnancy progressed and we decided then to delay the wedding. I was by now four months pregnant and my bump was small and barely noticeable, but to me I was huge. I wore loose clothing and the reality was that you couldn't really tell I was pregnant at all; cropped leggings and shell suits were all the rage at this time so the shell suit jackets covered my bump amazingly, but underneath all that I knew I had this tiny little person I loved with every breath I took, growing inside of me.

Words that could explain the feeling then and even now fail me as I know many mothers and mothers to be can understand.

A few weeks later I was now 20 weeks pregnant, time for scan number two. This time the blob looked more like a tiny person; we went together again and I was in awe of what I was seeing on the screen, but he appeared distant, uninterested even, not really looking or making any expression at this wonder on the screen in front of us. I was stunned – when had he changed? Did he no longer want our baby or was he just scared and the reality of the responsibility of being a parent becoming all too much? It was understandable; I too was scared, scared of labour, scared of getting it wrong, that I couldn't do it, that I would be a terrible mom, that I would fail miserably, and what if I didn't love my baby when it was born – never likely to happen I already loved this little one so much my heart ached at the thought of finally getting to hold my precious baby in my arms.

Two weeks later we had made plans; we were meant to go baby shopping, but I couldn't get hold of him. He didn't turn up for our pre-planned meeting, no one knew where he was, neither his parents nor friends had seen him; I was fraught with fear that something awful had happened to the father of my child. I knew he wasn't with his brother – he had split with his girlfriend, got into some trouble and moved to the Isle of Man where he had met a young girl, and apparently they had begun living together just a couple of months earlier. Where on earth was he? I contacted his mother and we got in her car, a Ford Capri, beige in colour with a dark roof, a classic car now. We drove around all the places we thought he may be, even some we guessed were unlikely, all to no avail.

The next couple of weeks I continued to contact his friends. I stayed with his parents in the hope of being there when news of his whereabouts came. Initially we were all terrified of what could have happened, but something changed; his mom didn't seem to be as concerned as I, no one had called the police to report him missing – okay he wasn't a child, but surely we needed to report him missing didn't we? I became increasingly suspicious – why had she not been as concerned, did she know something, had he just needed some time to get himself together, sort his thoughts and feeling out about the imminent parental responsibilities, had he fallen for another and out of love with me because my body was changing, did he no longer find me attractive? All sorts of thoughts had been plaguing my mind and preventing me from any sort of sleep. Eventually his mom broke down, she couldn't lie to me any longer. He was fine, he had called his mom and confessed that he had taken a flight to visit his brother on the Isle of Man to get his thoughts together. He had only planned to stay a short while, but some time in the past fortnight he had apparently met another girl, and he claimed he was in love and wasn't coming home. His mother was sobbing whilst telling me of his phone call; she hadn't known how to break it to me and was afraid of what may happen if I became increasingly upset or stressed. Became increasingly upset or stressed? I already was – he had been absent with no explanation for almost two weeks. I had been going out of my mind imagining all sorts of horrific things, and instead he had been living the high life with his brother, partying and had apparently meeting the love of his life, which he had said was me. Clearly he had been lying, hadn't he?

The news brought me to my knees. I was now more than five months' pregnant; I was still tiny, and my bump was easily disguisable, but I felt my tummy everyday. I was still in awe of this wonderful thing that was happening to me, and suddenly my world had been torn apart. Imagine a jigsaw puzzle showing the picture of the perfect family outside the perfect home with a beautiful green garden, children playing on the lawn, a white picket fence even, and the sun shining perfectly on the picture of hope and happiness. Now imagine someone crumpling that picture, all your hopes and dreams being crushed by that person's single action, destroying the picture perfect life, the house and family you dreamed of as a little girl. Now imagine you have swallowed the pieces of that puzzle. That's how it felt. I couldn't breathe, I couldn't swallow, the room begun to spin. What the hell just happened? Just a few months ago we were planning a wedding, a christening, our first home, the colour of our bedroom and the nursery; gender scans weren't around back then so boy or girl, it would be a surprise and I didn't care either way. I knew I would love it with all my heart. But now, today, all that was a distant memory, destroyed by one phone call and his mom's eventual admission of the truth.

I couldn't believe it was true, wouldn't accept that in that short space of time he had found another love and no longer felt love for me and our baby. I convinced myself he was just scared and running; I had to see him, make him realise that it would all be okay, that we would have the dream and be a happy little family unit, we could make it work, I knew we could. I had to tell my parents, I knew that, but how could I given how they despised him already, particularly my father. I could just see it now, my dad standing over me saying "I warned you, I knew he was bad from the start, but you wouldn't listen, would you?" I feared that smugness of his being right, of having to admit that despite my best efforts he really was no good. NO, I wasn't going to allow it, to accept it. I was going to find him and make him see sense and bring him home. When he saw me I was sure he would realise that I was still the 'love of his life'. My head was swimming with feelings and thoughts. I knew his mom would lend me the money for the flight, and she did although I hadn't given any thought to how I would repay her. I booked an open return flight that day and then headed home to pack and face the daunting task of telling my parents. I was heading to the airport and getting on an aeroplane, almost six months' pregnant, all alone with no idea where I was going. I had never been to the Isle of Man before. Would I even make it out of the airport when I landed? Where on earth I would I start my search?

My mother was furious, at me for even considering going, furious I was taking a flight all alone whilst I was pregnant and even more furious at his mother for giving me the funds to do so. I thought she was going to burst, she was so angry and upset. I couldn't bear to look at her, it broke my heart to be doing this to my mom. I knew the worry this would bring for her – her daughter and unborn grandchild travelling to an unknown place all alone, but I had to do it, for me, for our baby. If there was the slightest chance this was all a lie and that when he saw me he would realise and come home, it was worth taking the chance.

The following day I headed for the airport, just a small holdall contained the necessities. I hadn't planned on my being there long, a day or two maybe. The island wasn't that big, there couldn't be too many nightclubs and I knew that these were the most likely places to find him; surely I would locate him within a few days and then we would both return home together. That was the plan, a well laid out plan I thought, get there, do what I needed to and come home to put the jigsaw puzzle back together again, easy ... wasn't it?

It was the beginning of August and the weather was warm and the days were long. I would have the light nights on my side for my search. I was sure everything would be okay, but I was inwardly terrified; I had hidden my fear from my mother, I had oozed a bravado of confidence and independence when I left, when in reality I was scared beyond belief. All throughout the flight I kept asking myself what the hell was I doing, what had I been thinking when I boarded the aeroplane. I didn't know anyone, hadn't even booked a hotel, I had minimal funds on me and didn't know how I would afford a hotel or B&B let alone afford to eat and drink once I arrived. Could I find a hostel, would there be room? Would it be safe? I didn't just have myself to think of now I had my unborn child, this tiny little person who never asked to be conceived and would now be totally reliant upon me keeping them safe and warm and fed. Dear God, what was I doing? All these thoughts flooded my head continually making me feel giddy and nauseous. Would I just disembark into the airport terminal and book a return flight straight back? That would have been the most sensible thing to do, but this was me – as my mom said, 'the risk taker'. No, I wouldn't let my fears beat me, I would do what I set out to. I would find somewhere to stay first, then start the search; I would find him and then we could all go home together. Stay on track, I kept telling myself, you can do this, it will all be fine. I kept repeating the words in my head trying to convince myself my fears were unfounded and it was just nerves.

The flight was short and unremarkable. I remember sitting there looking out the window of the propeller-powered plane thinking it was a shed with wings; there were just five seats across, two one side three the other. The flight was relatively empty and I sat alone looking out of the windows, absorbed by all the notions and feeling swimming around my head, flooding out the hum of the plane. I just needed to get there, do what had to be done and come back home to the safety and comfort of my family and friends, with the father of my child, my fiancé.

We landed in a tiny airport. The terminal was small and it didn't take long before I was out of there. I stood for a while wandering which way to go; I was tired, it was hot and I was hungry and thirsty. I headed towards the exit signs, walking with a complete unawareness for anyone around me, concentrating on my own thoughts, and decided to head towards the nearest shopping centre.

I remember walking for what seemed like ages, not knowing what my next move was. I looked up from the pavement and was quickly distracted from my thoughts – was it really him? Was he just standing there slouched against the wall with no care in the world, smiling at me as if nothing was wrong? How dare he! I had been to hell and back the past few weeks, the worry, stress and upset he had caused. I wanted to punch him; fortunately I restrained myself and thankfully so – it was his twin brother, I realised as I got closer. Over the years I had learned to know their differences and could now tell them apart – not so easy in the beginning – and I certainly had a few pranks played on me by them both. I even verbally attacked his brother once when he had forgotten to meet me off the bus and I was walking down a quiet unlit route to his house alone, petrified, and then suddenly he was walking towards me. I met him with a barrage of angry words before finally realising it was the wrong twin and had to apologise profusely.

His brother greeted me with both surprise and concern. He had spoken with his mom and knew I was headed toward the island. We chatted a while and he avoided the subject of his brother, quickly changing the conversation to asking if I was OK. Was the baby OK? What was I doing there and where was I staying? To which I replied, "we're both OK under the circumstances," and to the last two questions the answer is the same, "I have no idea!" We met up with his relatively new girlfriend who was truly lovely; she lived alone with just her mom and offered for me to stay with her, which was a relief – at least that was one issue resolved and I had somewhere to stay. His brother said he had to work and that his girlfriend would look after me and he would see me later, and then swiftly left.

We chatted a while whilst we walked to her car. I was so relived and grateful at the offer of a place to stay and she seemed a genuinely nice person. I remember getting in the car and reaching for my seat belt, and Dawn looking at me and laughing, "What are you doing?" she asked. Unbeknown to me, although seatbelts had been compulsory since 1983 in England, they still weren't compulsory in the Isle of Man by 1990, and putting on a seat belt was the butt of much teasing during my stay. But I had to protect my precious load, so I wore it all the time anyway and took the jibes in my stride. When we arrived at her house her mother was extremely welcoming; she herself was a single mom and willingly agreed it would be OK for me to stay a few nights, but insisted I call my parents and let them know I was safe and where I was staying. We then had a cup of coffee and Dawn took me up to her room, which we would be sharing for a few nights. Her room was in the attic area of a quaint little house in Ballachurry; the room was small but it was cosy and I was not in a position to be choosy or picky. I just needed to get myself sorted now I had a base, and start my search.

Dawn had agreed to take me to look for my baby's father. She had lived on the island all her life, she drove, and she knew her way around. Being a small island with a population of around 69,000, little was kept secret for too long. She said she would take me to where I could find him, but first she needed to tell me something.

Apparently he had arrived on the island in pretty much the same manner as I – no clue where he was going or staying, just knowing he was visiting his brother; he had very quickly met up with a mixed race girl who was apparently from a relatively affluent family. He had immediately taken up with her and moved into her home. She would take me there, but wanted to prepare me for what I was about to see. I already knew he had met someone else from his mother; I needed to see it for myself and hear him say he didn't want us anymore. I needed closure no matter how painful and hurtful, so we headed off to find him.

We pulled up outside her house. It appeared to be a bungalow and the front door was raised from the road by steps. I sat in the car for a while wondering whether he would be there, what he would say when he saw me, and what would I say. And once again my head and stomach begun to turn in opposite directions like the well-oiled cogs in a piece of machinery. I was once again overcome with a flood of emotions; I had to tell myself to get a grip, this is what I came for, get it done and then we can all go home. With trembling knees and rising trepidation I opened the car door, putting one foot in front of the other. Walking in a straight line seemed to be a mammoth task in itself; I was willing myself along at each step. I stopped at the bottom of the stairs leading up to the front door, a pretty rockery and large boulders adorned the front garden. I looked at Dawn in the car and then back to the pretty borders of the garden and wondered how a home so pretty could maybe hold something so soul destroying. Come on, I thought, just a few steps to the front door. I willed myself along. I made it and stood there wondering how, and there I continued to stand, afraid to knock, afraid of what could be behind the door. Are they wrong? Please don't let it be true. I didn't want him to be there, I wanted it all to be just a terrible dream I would wake up from. I eventually knocked and waited – no answer – I knocked again and then noticed a slight movement of the curtain, so someone was definitely in. I knocked yet again; eventually the door began to open in what seemed like slow motion, and there he stood, topless, with anger all over his face. "Why are you here?" he said. I told him I needed to know, was it over? Was I to raise our baby alone? What had changed? I needed answers, I couldn't get closure without knowing. He told me he loved me, to go back with Dawn and he would be in touch; he was only staying with the girl because he had nowhere to go and she offered him a place to stay. I felt foolish, dumbfounded, and I think I must have turned and sprinted back to the car. I sat there trying to catch my breath. It was Thursday, it was August, it was hot and sunny and the heat and exhaustion only added to my nausea and giddiness. Dawn suggested we go out to a club that evening where she knew he would be so that I could see for myself if there really was anything going on. Later that evening we met up with some friends of Dawn's, all lovely people who welcomed me with open arms. Although I was almost 6 months' pregnant I could still easily hide my bump, and soon we were heading to the club.

We arrived early and the club was relatively empty. His brother had already arrived but the father of my baby was nowhere in sight. I was anxious and unable to settle; the friends we had come with were amazing and tried to keep my mind off matters and lift my spirits, which worked for a little while. Eventually he made his appearance with the girl. They seemed very close. The look on his face when he noticed me was a picture, and not a pretty one – I couldn't decide whether it was anger or concern that had his face all contorted. It was what felt like some considerable time before he eventually came to speak with me. He showed concern for me and the baby, asking why I was out in a club; he wasn't happy I was there – that was clearly evident – so the contortion had been both anger *and* concern, not one or the other, and I wasn't convinced that the concern was less for me and bump but more out of concern and embarrassment for himself. He said he would be coming home with me – that this was just something he needed to do – but he needed a few days to straighten things out with the girl he was with, as he had in essence used her for his stay and really loved me. The night went on with no further issues and I returned to Dawn's that evening.

Over the next few days we met and talked about things, it did appear that he genuinely wanted to come back with me and realised he had made a mistake in running away and trying to forget and carrying on with another girl. I booked my return flight for the end of the following week. During my stay on the Isle of Man I had met some wonderful people and made some great memories but knew I needed to go home and hopefully we would do so together. Dawn's mom had been an inspiration in the event that the jigsaw picture couldn't be rebuilt. She had raised Dawn on her own after Dawn's dad left when she was very young; they managed and she appeared happy with her life. Maybe there was a way to get through this on my own, although God willing, I wouldn't have to.

I also knew I had to get home as my brother was getting married on 18 August; both my sisters and the bride's sister were to be bridesmaids in large puffy peach dresses. As it was assumed that my pregnancy would be showing considerably by this time, I was unable to be a bridesmaid, but nonetheless I had to be home in time or my brother would never have forgiven me. We had always been close growing up and I needed to be there for him on his big day.

On my last evening we went to a club again. I remember 'Please don't go' by KLF being played and all the friends I had met during my stay gathered around me and started singing it to me. I was so grateful for their company and their uplifting words; they really did keep me sane during my week's stay, but my gratitude was mainly for Dawn and her mom. I prepared the next morning to go to the airport – Dawn was taking me and I was to meet with my baby's father at the airport. He had made plans to follow on the next available flight, but he didn't show at the airport, neither did he come home, eventually telling me that he had decided to stay on the Isle of Man and had no intention of coming home to me and our baby.

My trip had not yielded the outcome I had prayed for, but had brought me closure. Now I had to accept and face the future with my baby alone, once again scared, uncertain and alone. Surely things could only get better.

CHAPTER 3

Beginning of the end

I returned home to my parents' house, not to his parents, thankfully into the arms of my mother. It took days for me to come around from my trip and the realisation I was facing motherhood alone. I hadn't got much for the baby due to all the events of the last few months, and decided to concentrate on making sure I had all the necessities. I didn't know if my little cherub would be a boy or girl, so I bought white or mint and lemon vests and baby grows, sleepsuits, blankets, towels, bootees, scratch mittens and toiletries, nappies, a changing box, Moses basket and baby bath. I still hadn't decided on a pushchair, but his parents had offered to buy that. My parents had been wonderful and had helped me so much; Mom was great in helping me get things ready and we packed them all neat and tidy and wrapped in storage boxes under my bed.

The following weekend was my brother's wedding, He looked so handsome and the bride looked stunning, as did all the bridal party. I had managed to find a lilac trouser suit to wear, which was a loose short jacket with white lapels and shoulder pads. Once again it was difficult to tell I was pregnant, and I am sure many of the wedding guests to whom I was introduced as the groom's other sister wondered what I had done to be excluded from being a bridesmaid. As it goes I could quite easily have worn the peach dress and no one would have noticed, but when the wedding plans were underway no one could have predicted I would carry such a small bump.

Once again I felt isolated. My sisters and parents were all on the bridal table at the wedding breakfast and I was set aside with other guests and alone – a soon to be single mother, excluded from my brother's bridal party and feeling very isolated and down – but I tried not to let it show. I didn't want to ruin my brother's big day.

Since getting back for the Isle of Man I hadn't seen as much of his parents. Whether this was due to the awkwardness between us, their guilt over their son or my resentment of what their son had done, I never really knew, just that I was home more now than I had been for the past couple of years, back sharing a room with my sisters and well into the third trimester of my pregnancy.

I visited my midwife, Eileen at regular intervals. She

was gentle and lovely and I always stayed for a chat when the clinic wasn't too busy. She had been a midwife all her working life; she was short with a pretty face, her sister was a midwife there too, and they were both well suited to their chosen vocation. All seemed to be going well, and although my bump remained very tiny it was just assumed I was have having a small baby. I thought this was OK and would probably mean an easy labour. I was only small myself at 5' 2" and hadn't been a big baby: born weighing 7lbs 10oz I had been the smallest of my mother's offspring, my younger brother being the biggest weighing a whopping 10lb 13oz and all the others had been between 9 and 10 pounds.

Things took a downturn when I was 28 weeks' pregnant, and I started to bleed. I was home and my mom called the GP out to see me. He advised bed rest and to keep my legs elevated – and for once I did as I was told. Mom kept telling me I needed to rest and that all the stress and upset had brought this about; I felt guilty for having possibly put my baby's health and safety at risk, chasing the dream that would never now be.

I spent the next two weeks at home on bed rest. I had been signed off from work due to stress some time ago and now it seemed unlikely I would return to work before the arrival of my tiny little one, although I didn't have much money or savings. I now needed to focus on making sure I kept my baby safe, and despite feeling devastated and alone and scared of being a single mom,

I had to consider another life now – no more was it just about me. I had a precious load to protect and care for now and forever.

Mom worked full time but didn't start work until 10am. She had worked part time up until a few years before when both my younger siblings had gone to school full time, and then she increased her hours. Dad was a postman and home by midday most of the time, so at least I had company for most of the day. It worked well for my parents, as Mom could be there before school and Dad would be there after school. During the holidays Mom would try to start later, and she and Dad would swap roles in caring for my siblings when he came home. I had lost touch with most of my friends, except one school friend with whom I had rekindled our relationship in 1989. It was now the latter part of 1990, mobile phones were only just becoming available to the general consumer and not many people could afford them; computers were for the rich and rare in schools; where there were computers they only used the DOS operating system, which meant black screens with green block characters; there were no email or social media accounts so most communication was face to face or via a landline, and then it was always by good luck getting through on the landline at my house – with five children the phone was rarely on the hook.

The bleeding eventually stopped. I went for a check-up at the midwife and they kept changing my due dates, saying my dates were wrong and I wasn't as far gone as they thought. This seemed odd as I was certain of my last period, but I just accepted what they said while in my own mind my due date didn't change. I knew I was certain of my dates and stuck with my own time schedule; I knew I was counting down the days.

My forever friend, Hazel, already had a little girl and a flat of her own, although she was no longer with the father of her daughter either. It seemed as though times were changing, and being a single parent was no longer the rarity it once was. Hazel and I kept each other company; when her daughter had been young she had stayed with me at our parents for a while and we had all helped her. She didn't really have anyone else to help – her mom and dad had divorced years earlier and her mom now lived more than 40 miles away with her younger sister. Despite remarrying it didn't work out either and her mom was now a single parent too. Neither Hazel nor her mom drove so it was difficult for them to see much of one another; she had an older sister but they didn't seem to have a great sister relationship even though they lived relatively close to one another. We had become like sisters over the decade we had been friends. I would often stay at her flat and many times got into her daughter's play pen with her daughter and played; there is a photo of me at about 32 weeks' pregnant sat in her play pen with a bucket on my head. I was wearing white dungarees with orange flowers on them – they do sound awful now, but they were great at the time and very comfortable. I was nearing the end and starting to accept I was going to have to do it alone, although not totally. I had my friend and family, and I would get by.

The following week I went to see Eileen my midwife for a check-up. I felt fine; my ankles were very swollen but weren't causing me any concern, and a lot of pregnant women suffer oedema when pregnant, especially in the latter stages.

We went through all the usual ante natal checks and at the end of the check-up the midwife told me she was sending me to the hospital. My blood pressure was high, I had swelling and there was protein in my water – all signs of pre-eclampsia. My heart was racing – how could this happen? I had been careful and sensible since the bleed five weeks ago. I didn't really understand the seriousness of the diagnosis – it wasn't possible to Google it back then. Today there is a lot more information available and everyone is much better informed, but I was pretty much in the dark about it back then.

I went home, packed a bag, and on 17 October 1990 I made my way to the hospital with my mom. I thought I may be in for a night or two and then be allowed home; it never occurred to me I may have to stay for weeks as it turned out I did.

The days felt long and the nights even longer. I was eventually moved into my own side room after about a week and told I would be scanned every week to check the baby's' progress. I was bored and lonely; family and friends visited whenever they could but it was no fun, and my blood pressure wasn't really settling so I couldn't go home. One day I popped my head into the side room next door, and to my pleasant surprise the young girl in there was known to me. Her name was Shelley; she was a couple of years older than me and had gone to school with my brother. She had been brought in for the same reasons I had. We chatted and became friends – we helped pass the time for one another. We were similar in height and colouring and on more than one occasion the staff got us mixed up; we found it amusing and they even brought the wrong medication to us on a few occasions so we had to swap them with one another.

My mom would bring me cheese and pickle crusty cobs when she visited me – it was my craving – and Shelley's mom would bring her one can of Guinness. She always defended it saying it was to help increase her iron intake as her iron levels were low. We shared stories and kept each other up on our down days; I was one week ahead and we knew potentially we could have our babies together. We were both so excited about the prospect of becoming a mom. Shelley was also facing becoming a single mom, and we spent endless hours walking up and down the ward chatting and listening to the radio at the nurses' station playing the latest hit records. Beautiful South's 'A Little Time' and the

Righteous Brothers' 'Unchained Melody' were played almost every time we were near the nurses' station, and I think eventually we both pretty much knew the lyrics off by heart. We got to know the staff and some of the other patients quite well during our time on the ward, although many of the patients were only short stays, either due to pre-natal issues or being in labour.

On 29 October 1990, my blood pressure went through the roof. I was suddenly whisked off to the labour ward, hooked up to machines and had a catheter inserted; my blood pressure had become so dangerously high that it was life threatening to both baby and me. I called my mom to let her know, as they thought they may have to deliver the baby early if my blood pressure didn't settle down soon.

I was kept on the labour ward all that night attached to a machine monitoring baby's heartbeat and my blood pressure.

Sometime during the night I felt a sudden gush of water. I turned and the nurse was next to me. I remember asking her if the catheter had come out or been removed, but she didn't seem concerned and didn't check. She just assured me everything was OK. A doctor came around sometime during the night and checked the baby's heart monitor print outs – they looked like a zig zag line. I heard him speak with the on duty midwife and refer to them as 'type two', but he said nothing more and left. By morning my blood pressure had come down, still high but no longer in the critical area, so I was transferred back to my room on the ward. Once again back with my friend and ordered to stay on bed rest. I had been scanned regularly up to now due to my baby being small, but each time I was told everything was normal, and that my dates must be wrong. I knew they weren't but didn't argue. The consultant came to see me when I returned to the ward and I asked when I would be scanned again; obviously I was anxious and concerned following the visit to the labour ward. He advised it wouldn't be for another two weeks, and when I queried this as he had previously said I would be scanned weekly, he said that they had no availability for the scanner, they were underfunded and couldn't procure a new scan machine, and the ones they had were already over booked. But he assured me all was fine, and that my concerns were normal for a first time mom-to-be. I would be scanned again in two weeks, which would be three weeks from the last scan.

When Mom came to see me that evening she animatedly told me what had happened that day at the post office. She had left home to go shopping, but first she went to collect her family allowance from the local post office counter – back then you had to queue on your allocated day to collect family allowance, it wasn't automatically paid into any bank account.

As Mom was leaving the post office she was approached by a Gipsy traveller. In those days we were all wary of any Gipsy; we had some notion that if you were disrespectful at all you may be cursed somehow, and therefore you never ignored a Gipsy.

The Gipsy had held Mom's hand and said to her, "Bonfire Night will go with a bang this year." Mom had bought the lavender she offered and parted company, sure that the Gipsy had meant I wouuld deliver my little one, her first grandchild, on Bonfire Night. The eerie thing about that is it would mean three generations having been born on memorable calendar dates: my mom was born on April Fool's Day, I was born on New Year's Eve and, if the Gipsy was right, my baby would arrive on Bonfire Night. No chance of anyone forgetting our birthdays!

Fortunately for Shelley she had been scanned that week; unfortunately this had only heightened her concerns. She was told that her baby wasn't growing and the hospital were suggesting she may need to deliver her baby early. All in all things weren't improving for either of us, and our anxiety levels were rising like tidal waves – soon the levels would peak, bringing about a tsunami of fear. On Friday 2 November, a doctor came around to see us both and much to our surprise told Shelley and I that we could go home for the weekend, but we were to be back on the ward early Monday morning. Shelley was refusing to go; she had been told about the baby's growth issues at her scan just that week and really didn't want to leave the hospital. She was fraught with desperation and trepidation and trying to convince the medical staff that she needed to stay; she was so scared something may happen and she wouldn't be in the best place for care. I too mirrored the same concerns, but our pleas fell on deaf ears. We were only told that there was no immediate danger to us and our babies, and that a few days at home with our families would be good therapy and prepare us both for the imminent arrival of our little ones. We both knew that when we came back we wouldn't be leaving the ward again without our babies, and as we had no choice other than to leave our hospital rooms as instructed by the doctors, we resigned ourselves to the fact that the weekend would be spent by both of us preparing everything that we needed to be ready for the arrival of our little cherubs. Reluctantly we packed up for the weekend and left the hospital bound for home.

Arriving home to my parents' house was such a relief. Although I had let the baby's father's parents know I had been in hospital, he never came to see me and neither did they. In all honesty, although I hoped in my heart that he would, my head knew he wouldn't. The first night at home was strange and yet comforting; sleeping in my own bed, spending time washing and getting things ready for the arrival of my baby, making sure I was counting my movements as always to make sure I was getting the normal ten per day; I was excited and nervous. I knew that anytime soon I would hold this little person that had stolen my heart from the very moment I had seen a blob on the scanner screen. Sunday came and the family had Sunday lunch together as always, apart from my eldest brother – he is two years older than I and now being married and living with his wife in their first home together very rarely came to Sunday lunch. Although I missed him, in some ways it was a blessing, as if you didn't eat quickly enough he would pinch bits off your plate, especially the Yorkshire pudding. My brother and his wife had bought a little semi-detached house not far from our parents, and I was pretty sure they too would have their first child soon enough.

The day was a typical Sunday. Spending time with my family was always a little chaotic; my sisters were two and twelve years younger than me and my other brother nine years younger, so there were always youngsters in the house and plenty going on. Later that evening I mentioned to my mom that I didn't think I had felt ten movements yet that day. Mom had said that it's not unusual for baby to go a little quiet before they are ready to make an appearance, and I was going back in a few hours anyway. I did call the midwife just to be sure, but was told they didn't think it was of significant concern, so I settled back into my Sunday evening at home to enjoy the TV. On Sunday evenings *London's Burning* was showing, one of my favourite programmes at that time. A fire woman had joined the team and had rescued a baby from a burning car just moments before it exploded; my heart had been racing watching it, and I was elated she had saved the tiny baby. I think we all eventually went up to bed around 11pm that night. I had my bags packed in the hall ready to go back to the ward, and everything was now ready at home for the arrival of my little one. Knowing I had fully prepared everything, I went to sleep feeling happy with the knowledge that the next time I would be at home sleeping in my bed, I would have my baby in my arms.

At around 3am I woke with excruciating pains in my stomach. I screamed out for my mom. I was in labour – what timing – my waters hadn't broken yet but the contractions were about every 6–7 minutes. Mom called an ambulance as no one had a car, and we were advised it would be with us shortly. Three hours later the ambulance arrived and eventually we were on our way to the hospital. Very soon my baby son or daughter would make their first appearance in this world; it was 5 November, and it seemed the Gipsy was to be right.

We arrived at the hospital and I was taken straight to the delivery suite; everything was ready and the midwife got all the paperwork sorted and went to fetch the heart monitor machine. When she came back she put the belts around me and moved the discs over my tummy into several different places, but couldn't seem to find a heartbeat. She wasn't concerned; she said sometimes during labour baby moves too much or too low for the discs to latch on to a continuous reading of the baby's heartbeat. So she went off to get a horn; these were used to listen to the heartbeat mostly by community midwives then. When she returned she placed the horn on my tummy, again moving it around into several different places, then she left the room without a word to me. I remember lying there wondering what was happening. Several minutes later she returned with a doctor. The midwife stood to my left side and held my hand, looking at me with pity in her eyes. Why? The doctor came around the bed with the horn and listened to my tummy. He seemed to be listening for a while before he finally stood up and returned to the base of my bed; he looked at me and said something. The wall behind him was a pale colour, almost white; there were no pictures, it was devoid of any distinguishable marks. He stood in front of it in his white coat, stethoscope hanging loosely around his neck, ID badge attached to his pocket. His coat was open and he had a nondescript pale blue shirt on. I cannot recall if he had a tie. He asked me if I had heard him. I had, I knew I had, but I couldn't believe what I thought I was hearing. It couldn't be possible, couldn't be true – they had to check again, maybe their machine or horn was faulty? Maybe they weren't doing the heart beat check properly. This wasn't happening, they were wrong, everything was OK, and in a few hours I would be holding my baby.

That moment in time would remain etched into my memory from that moment on, forever my waking dream, my worst nightmare a reality, the thing that should never happen to me, to anyone.

The next 12 hours were a blur. The labour stopped and I had to be induced, prolonging the agony. The trauma that both my mind and body were going through was completely unimaginable – knowing that it wouldn't end with tears of joy but tears of despair and heartbreak. I was merely existing, I wasn't alive. A part of me had died with my baby, and now my baby didn't want to leave me and I didn't want it to go. Eventually the physical pain ended but the emotional pain had only just begun. I had a baby daughter weighing just 2lb 4oz, with a mass of jet black hair and the tiniest fingers and toes ever imaginable. Her lips were cherry red – caused by oxygen starvation I later discovered. She was handed to me swaddled in a white shawl; nothing I had would have fitted her, she was like a tiny doll. My baby, my little girl, hadn't been born into my arms but into the arms of Jesus. The Gipsy had been right. Bonfire Night had certainly gone with a bang, and not the sort I ever imagined.

The head of midwifery at the hospital at that time, Lesley, had delivered my younger siblings, and both she and her husband Terry had become family friends. She had sat with me all through the labour and brought my daughter into the world. I was grateful that she had been carefully and tenderly delivered by someone I knew and cherished and not a stranger. I knew Lesley would take good care of her for me. After the birth I spent some time with my little girl and named her Jade. She looked so peaceful. I had been given some strong pain killers and I was drowsy, but I held her for as long as I could, as long as I could stay awake. I didn't want to let her go. She was so tiny and helpless; how could I have let her down so badly? My heart ached beyond any pain imaginable and I wanted to keep her wrapped in my arms forever. I must have dozed off from the medication I had been given, and when I awoke I was no longer holding her. My arms felt empty and lifeless; where was she? I tried to get up off the bed – I had to find her – but I couldn't move. My body stiffened with fear – someone had stolen my baby. I became uncontrollably inconsolable and I was subsequently given more medication; with this I slipped back into unconsciousness.

It was later, when I came around again, that Mom told me where Jade was. She said Jade was in a special room, and both she and my sister had been to see her and held her and that she was fine and being looked after. In reality she wasn't fine, I wasn't fine, and nothing ever would be fine ever again.

CHAPTER 4

Home alone

Later that day I was taken back to the same room I had spent the last three weeks in. It was evening by this time and still Bonfire Night; soon the sky would be alight with displays of gunpowder and flashing colours, and the smell in the air and the sounds from the fireworks displays would, from this day on, be a constant reminder of my loss. I felt dead inside. I stood at the window of my room overlooking the cemetery next door. It was a view I'd had for the past few weeks, and it had never appeared morbid; somehow it always looked peaceful, with a beautiful arrangement of trees and well-tended headstones always awash with colour. That was my view again today.

The door to my room opened and Shelley came in. I knew it was her but I didn't want to look – how could I? My baby had died. But she already knew – the ward staff had told her – and then I suddenly remembered and realised what I had been told. Shelley had lost her baby too, just hours before me on the evening of Sunday, 4 November. I turned and looked at her, eyes all red and swollen, and we hugged for ages. The previous evening she had returned early to the hospital, concerned for her baby as her movements had also been slow throughout Sunday. Tragically she had lost her baby, a daughter. She had been alone the evening before in her room, contemplating my return the next day and dreading seeing me, thinking I would still have my baby and she wouldn't have hers. Then early in the morning on 5 November a member of the nursing team had come into her room and told her I was on the labour ward. Shelley was distraught from her loss and wondering how she would face me when I returned to the ward with my baby, as we had witnessed many mothers previously while on the ward, which was mixed pre- and post-natal care at the time. Around mid-morning Shelley was given the news that I had lost my baby, and she was filled once again not only with her own grief but also feeling mine. Once I first came around from the sedation and became remotely coherent and able to understand what was being said, I remembered that I had been told Shelley had lost her baby the previous night. We were both filled with a double sense of loss.

Somehow, through our loss, we found peace in one another. We shared our grief, frustrations and heartache; we were now soul mates forever joined through our loss. Our baby girls had come into this world and left together, and now we were left together to try to find a way to deal with our tragedies. We would not get over the loss, we knew that, but we also knew we had to find a way to learn to live each day, and together we had an indescribable and unwritten understanding of one another.

That night, after our visitors had left – not that we had had many words for them, neither of us had, we'd both sat in silence or just sobbed – we sat each in our own room with our own thoughts. We hadn't been allowed home and part of me didn't want to leave – how could I go home and leave my baby girl here? It wasn't right, it wasn't just. I sat and the tears kept falling, each tear a little memory of the time I carried her in my tummy, thinking I was keeping her safe when all the time I was failing her. The fireworks lit up the skies in an amazing display of shapes and colours, like stars falling from above, disappearing before they landed. The clouds seemed so still and lifeless, just like me. They seemed to engulf the orange-tinted skyline, and I sat wishing I could fly up past those clouds, get on that stairway to heaven and hold my little girl once again. I stared for hours out of the window, scared to sleep, scared of what my dreams would bring to me – the white room, the white coat, those words, "I am afraid your baby has died," would be forever engraved in my memory.

Not managing to sleep at all that night, I lay on my bed trying to block out the sounds of the comings and goings on the ward. There always seemed a lot of hustle and bustle but tonight more so than usual, or maybe it was just that the sounds appeared even more profound right now. Once the fireworks ceased, the cries of a new born baby could be heard even though the door to my room, which had been kept tightly closed. The screams of labour and cries of new babies seemed to only ring louder; I pushed my fingers deep into my ears but the sounds wouldn't go away. I am not sure whether there was just one baby born that night and maybe the repetitive sounds were just an echo in my head, but all I know is that they seemed to go on continuously and no matter what I did I could not drown out the resounding noise of a new born baby's cry. Every second felt like a crushing punishment; I curled into a foetal position wanting to protect myself from the sounds, praying it would stop. No more was the memory of the sweet humming of a radio at the nurses' station, just a constant reminder of what I would never hear from my little girl – never hear her cries, her laughter, her sweet voice. I wished for a moment I was unable to hear anything, that way I wouldn't have the crushing realisation that I had not heard my baby's first cry.

Neither Shelley nor I had left our hospital rooms other than to see one another since returning from the labour ward, and we hadn't even gone for any meals. We knew exactly when it was meal time, as by now we were used to the smells that permeated through the ward. At that time there was a dining room on the ward, and those patients able to walk and get around would go to the dining room for their meals. We hadn't wanted to eat anyway, but the smells reminded us what time of day it was as meal times were set, and we were fully aware of other patients walking down the ward to get their food. We couldn't face them. Some had been on the ward long enough for us to have got to know them, and we knew that they would still have their babies. Just the thought of seeing another pregnant woman and someone cradling their baby filled me with a cocktail of emotions that exploded in tears of anguish, wanting to be in the room we had spent the last few weeks in as it offered a sense of security, and yet not wanting anyone else to be there on the ward. Just putting one foot to the floor was exhausting in itself; talking and explaining to anyone was not even in my sights right then.

The following morning Shelley and I talked for ages and coerced one another into going together to the dining room to get some breakfast. Neither of us relished the thought, but together we had decided that it was the first step to take and we would have one another to hold onto. Walking to the dining room took every ounce of energy we could muster up; we clung on to each other as if we would fall into some deep dark hole that we would never come up from if we let go. As we approached the room, Tina, a patient we had become acquainted with just a few days prior to our tragedies, and who was still blooming, came bouncing over to us, clearly noticing the absence of our large bumps. With an excited edge to her voice she almost sang her words, "Oh my god ladies, what did you have?" Shelley and I stood still, our eyes facing the floor, hearts beating faster than the engine of a Formula One racing car, Tina's words resonating in my ears. The floor began to spin; I held on to Shelley's arm with all the strength I had. I could envisage that deep dark hole and wanted to just fall right into it at that moment and never return, never have to reply to her question. It felt as if we were stood unable to move for a lifetime when in reality it was seconds. Neither of us managed to make a sound, not even a squeak. We just turned and went back to my room and sat on my bed holding each other, crying relentlessly. No words were needed – we understood one another – all we had and needed now was each other; consumed by grief, bonded in tragedy, forever soul mates.

For the next two days we talked endlessly about our loss and how we would cope when we went home without our daughters. Word eventually spread throughout the patients and staff; the staff were supportive and the pity in their eyes was apparent each time they came into our rooms. We did eventually make our way to the breakfast room the following day, and the patients who knew us, including Tina, by now knew of our loss and each one expressed their sorrow. Each pregnant woman I saw felt like another stab in the heart, but it wasn't their fault, and I prayed over each one for the healthy and safe arrival of their baby. I would never wish what Shelley and I were going through upon my worst enemy. It's not natural for any parent to have to contemplate living – if they can, existing, if not – without their child. I prayed too that I could get up each day. The sleeping pills had aided some sleep but it was artificially induced. I wondered what normal would be like now. I knew for sure that what I thought previously was normal was never going to be that way again.

Eventually, Shelley and I packed up our things, desperately trying to deal with the notion that we would be leaving without our babies. I felt I just couldn't go; how could I leave here? My baby girl was still there and I was deserting her; I was leaving the hospital, going home and she was staying. I was still coming to terms with what had happened. Eventually, after much coercion, I left the hospital in a state of numbness. Walking out of the metal framed glass doors of the maternity block I felt nothing, completely detached from reality and people. Suddenly the world had lost all its colour, all its meaning, and I knew I was leaving behind a part of me that had also died that day and would cease to exist forever.

Lesley pulled up outside the maternity unit and took my mom and I home. I kept looking back – everything felt surreal – how could I be leaving without her? What would I do when I arrived home to my parents? I couldn't breathe. I closed my eyes and prayed, prayed it wasn't true, prayed I would wake up from this terrible nightmare, prayed I would hold my little girl again soon, prayed for a time when this would never happen to anyone ever again. I just kept my eyes closed and prayed all the way back.

I walked into the house. I could sense the atmosphere but didn't want to be around anyone and went to my room; I looked under my bed for the tubs where I had lovingly placed all I had bought for my daughter, Jade Natasha. I had known from the start that if I had a daughter I would call her Jade; her middle name came to me after I had held her, from where I don't know. It had no relevance, I just liked how it sounded and it seemed to suit her.

It was empty. Under my bed was empty. Where was it all, where had everything gone? I screamed in sheer terror and frustration – who had taken my baby's things? It turned out my mom had removed everything for fear it would upset me – she had apparently been advised that taking it out of sight would be for the best and she thought she was doing the right thing. She was looking out for me but right then, at that moment, I felt a surge of feelings I had never before felt for my mother. I wanted to scream and shout at her, to scratch her eyes out – how could she, how dare she? They weren't her things, they were mine, my daughter's. At that moment I could feel nothing but anger, anger at the hospital, at the doctors, at the nurses, at the ambulance for taking so long to fetch me that night, at my mom for taking my things, at the world for continuing to live when I no longer felt I had a reason to. The numbness had been replaced by a sense of anguish and anger that was out of my control. I didn't even consider what my mom must have been going through – she had lost her granddaughter and her daughter was losing her mind – how painful it must have been for my mother to have to watch her child going through such anguish and feeling totally useless. There was nothing she could do, nothing would bring my daughter, her granddaughter, her first grandchild, back and she had to watch me curl over in pain, going from a deranged woman to a sobbing little girl, looking for someone, anyone, to blame and lashing out at the ones closest. Seeing me with empty eyes and struggling to find a reason to live, seeing your child give up on life, must be an horrendous ordeal for any parent.

I later discovered that Shelley's parents had done the same, although they had placed all the items, wrapped inside the baby bath, into their attic. Shelley hadn't said anything to her parents, and a part of me wished I had stayed silent too. My mom didn't deserve the wrath I had bestowed upon her when I found all my baby things gone, but I had been unable to control the torrent of anger that had surged through my body at that moment, a moment I would probably recall many times.

For all of the next week I sat in silence; I didn't eat and refused to speak. Lesley had been to seen me a few times with Terry, her husband who had once been an ambulance man and was now a funeral director. Terry was going to take care of my little Jade Natasha and make all the arrangements; how ironic that Lesley had helped bring Jade into the world and Terry would now take care of her departure. Before any arrangements could be made I needed to first register the birth and death. The hospital had given me a death certificate but I still needed to take it to the registrar office to have it legally registered. I refused point blank; doing so would be admitting that she was gone, and I wasn't ready for that. Shelley had made all her arrangements and her daughter's funeral, which was to take place on 15 November, and her burial plot was all arranged. Not mine, not my little girl's. I was not doing it, I just couldn't.

'Unchained Melody' by the Righteous Brothers was top of the charts still, and I knew this would be my song for Jade. It epitomised all I felt and wanted to say, and each time I heard it playing on the radio in the kitchen at home I cried some more, more than I already was or thought I could. I would sit on the sofa and hear the soft tune playing in the background – even when it wasn't on the radio it kept playing in my head. I had heard it so many times in the hospital, but hearing it now it took on a totally different meaning; no longer did it feel like a sentimental love song, now it had become a eulogy for my little angel.

> *Whoa, my love, my darling*
> *I hungered for your touch*
> *A long, lonely time*
> *And time goes by so slowly*
> *And time can do so much*
> *Are you still mine*
> *I need your love*
> *I need your love*
> *God speed your love to me*
> *Lonely rivers flow to the sea, to the sea*
> *To the open arms of the sea*
> *Lonely rivers sigh "wait for me, wait for me*
> *I'll be coming home wait for me"*

I was sitting in my now usual place, on the sofa in the lounge, when on this particular day my dad walked in and, saying nothing, simply placed a brown paper bag next to me and left the room. No one knew what to say; there wasn't a right or wrong thing that could be said. I felt alone and wanted to be left alone. After a while I picked up the paper bag and looked inside. There was a colouring book and felt tips pens inside. As a child I had always loved to colour; my parents both knew and had obviously remembered; not knowing what else to, and even though I was a few weeks off turning 20 years old, they had gone to the shops and bought the only thing I had always loved as a child – a colouring book. I opened the book and began to colour. I coloured for hours, days even; I found it took my mind away from reality, gave my emotional cortex some respite and my tear ducts some much needed rest – except when I heard 'Unchained Melody', and then the tears and the visions popped back into my head, and occasionally the colours would merge from the stain of my teardrops on the pages of the book.

A week after coming home, Terry called to see me. He came up to my parents' room where I had been sleeping with my mom since I had left the hospital – my dad had taken up residence at night in the lounge – and asked me about funeral arrangements. I refused to discuss it. Terry had known me since I was a little girl; in fact it was he who eventually got me to give up my dummy before I turned three years old. We were visiting Terry and Lesley at their flat at the time, and he took my dummy and threw it over the balcony – or so he had me believe as a toddler. In reality he had given it to my mom, but she never told me she had it and never gave it to me again. It sounds like an horrific ordeal, but for the sake of my teeth I am sure he did me a favour. Terry gave me a stern talking to, saying that whilst he understood what I was feeling, I wasn't considering my daughter, leaving her alone in the funeral home waiting to be put to rest. He couldn't do anything, make any arrangements until I had registered her death. I knew it made sense; I was being selfish leaving her all alone because I couldn't and wouldn't accept what needed to be done. I eventually agreed and, as promised, did as I said I would. Finally her funeral was arranged for Tuesday 20 November 1990, less than a week after Shelley was to bury her daughter. We had both opted for burial; neither of us could face the thought of a cremation.

I had refused until now to contact the Stillbirth and Neonatal Death (Sands) charity to speak to someone, but one evening a volunteer from Sands called me. At first I wouldn't come to the phone, but out of politeness for the caller – as this was how I had been raised, to be respectful and polite always – I eventually did, and I was glad I had. Suddenly everything started to flow out of my mouth; I found the ability to string a sentence together that day for the first time since Bonfire Night; all that I had been holding in and refusing to say for fear of having to accept reality, suddenly just gushed from me. I sat and talked to them for what seemed like an eternity. I was given the name of a support contact and a few days later I received a lovely hand written letter from the volunteer about our chat and newsletters the charity had that I should read. I was truly grateful for their insistence and support, and for just listening. The volunteer had experienced tragedy too, and so was a great listener and understood my emotions and actions.

That same week the vicar came to see me. I had decided Jade should be buried in the cemetery next to the hospital, because it had never seemed a sad and frightening place whilst it had been my view from my hospital room, and it was filled with beautiful greenery. The vicar explained that as my daughter was being buried on holy grounds, he would first conduct her baptism/christening before commencing with the funeral service. The thought of sitting through two services filled me with dread. I am certain at that moment my heart stopped beating for a second and I wished it wouldn't beat again, that I could be with my little girl. We could be together, mommy and daughter, forever together.

It felt as though my head would explode; there were so many unanswered questions. How could I ever get an answer and know what had gone wrong? Why was I arranging the funeral of my child, my first born, my little girl?

Lesley had suggested I focus my pent up anger on the pursuit of some answers and that I write a letter to my consultant in preparation for my follow up appointment at the hospital. Nothing would ever bring my daughter back, but I needed to know the answers to some of my questions. And so, I focused my attention on the hospital and the consultant; someone needed to provide some clarification, some answers, some reasoning why my baby girl was gone!

13 November 1990

Dear Mr Crawford

I am writing to you with regards to the events leading up to the stillbirth of my baby. I'm afraid there are so many questions that I feel have been left unanswered. I'm finding it very hard to accept what has happened because of this, and so many people tell me you are the only one who can answer the following questions.

1. *Why, when blood tests were being taken to test the placenta, was I not told the results? From the state of the placenta at birth it obviously hadn't been very good for a while.*

2. *When I was in labour the midwife found the membranes had previously ruptured. The only time I had the feeling I couldn't hold my water was over a week previous to the birth, which was the Monday night I was taken to the labour ward and had a catheter. Not knowing exactly what the catheter was or did I just presumed it had come away. The midwife on duty at the time checked and didn't say anything, but after recently making enquiries about a catheter I have found it could not have caused such a loss of water, so it seems that my waters actually broke a week previous to the birth of my baby girl, Jade, and yet nothing was done and everything was left.*

3. *The Monday I refer to above, the doctor on duty*

referred to the drops on the baby heart beat monitor as 'type two' which I have recently discovered means the drops in my baby's heart beat were occurring at the end of contractions. Taking into consideration that my baby wasn't growing, I can't understand why she couldn't have been delivered at this time. I appreciate that this wouldn't necessarily have meant she would have survived, but at least she would have been given a chance.

4. *Why, after being monitored every day, sometimes more than once a day for long periods, was the monitoring suddenly stopped the Wednesday before Jade was born?*

5. *Why was I told it was OK for me to go home for the weekend, that things were looking up, when it's obvious now that everything wasn't alright?*

6. *The first week I was admitted you came to see me on the Friday and said that you would scan me again next week. I had already been scanned during that week, and you said that if the baby wasn't growing at all you would, in your words, 'get it out'. But when you came to see me the following Friday, you said that you wouldn't scan me again for another two weeks and that I could go home for the weekend even though the scans had been showing my baby wasn't growing. When I asked why I was being left another two weeks I was told it was because you really needed at least*

two weeks to see any growth, and when I asked why I then couldn't be scanned the following week as that would have been the two weeks, I was told that you had to cut back on the use of the scanner.

7. *Why did you suddenly change your mind about delivering my baby when you were aware she wasn't growing?*

I have been given an appointment to attend your clinic on December 19 1990 at 9.40am. I look forward to seeing you then so that you can answer the above questions and then I will be able to hopefully understand what went wrong.

Yours sincerely,

After sending the letter, I also decided I would start fundraising for a new scanner machine for the hospital, in the hope that it may prevent any other mother suffering a tragedy due to the lack of resources and funds. Lesley agreed to help me with this and made the first donation to start me off.

Nothing would ever bring my baby back or make me feel better, but if I could do something, anything, to stop this happening to someone else and feeling the bottomless pain I did, then I would do it.

CHAPTER 5

Funeral

The funeral had been arranged. I had chosen a white marble casket with tiny silver handles, and Lesley had made a perfectly sized white satin dress with peach trimmings and a bonnet to match for my Jade to wear. I had purchased two silver bangles and had them engraved with her name 'Jade'. One would stay with me, and the other would go into the casket with my little girl. I arranged for white and peach flowers in the shape of a teddy bear and also had a teddy placed in her casket so she wouldn't be alone.

I hadn't heard anything from her dad since I had left the Isle of Man, and despite all the issues I had with the pregnancy and the time I had spent in hospital I had not heard nor seen much from his parents; it seemed that they had all just forgotten.

As I prepared for what would undoubtedly be the worst day of my life, I decided I would write a letter for my precious Jade Natasha, my peachy skinned, red lipped, dark haired tiny angel. I thought I might read it at the funeral, but decided I couldn't do it and didn't want to have anyone else read it instead. I tried to sit and write but couldn't find the words. I wrote the first line and seemed to sit and stare at the page for ever; how could any words describe what I was feeling, how my world had changed forever? Nothing would ever be the same. I sat and stared at the piece of paper with just one line written on it, and then I started to write almost as if I wasn't even thinking, and my letter became a poem. This would be my special message to my baby girl; I would read it to her in my prayers and hope she would hear me.

We had such little time together before God made us part
But Jade, my little darling, you'll be forever in my heart
I wish that I could tell you all the things you ought to know
Like how my love for you will never cease to grow
If there were something I possessed would have meant you'd live
My life, my heart, my soul, I surely would have give
I wish that I could hold you in my arms just once again
Knowing that I can't, causes me much pain
But Jade you'll always be my little girl so dear
And in my heart and thoughts you'll stay forever and a year.

Suddenly the words kept flowing, all in the form of short poems, as if someone else was directing the pen. I just kept writing.

God gave you to me then took you away
For what reason I cannot say
But Jade what I'd give to have you back
Though to create a miracle this ability I lack
I wish little star that God above
Had let you live for me to love
I wish in my arms that you could be
Your loving eyes for me to see
Those cherry red lips and dark brown hair
Your laughter and tears I long to share
I love you Jade with all my heart
It hurts to think we're so far apart
Be patient little one for one day we'll be
Together again just wait and see.

I knew from this moment on that this was how I would express what I felt for Jade. I called her my little star, and I would go outside at night to look at the sky, just as I had since Bonfire Night. I would seek out the brightest star and know that was my little girl who got her angel wings too soon. I would stare at that star for ages and silently speak with her. I prayed she would hear me; I needed to believe she could.

Friends had been to see me since I had come home, but every visit just brought a silence. No one knew what to say and I couldn't find my voice to speak. I was sure the visitors would soon wane as word got around how painful seeing me was for anyone; one of my close friends couldn't even find the courage to come alone and brought two other girlfriends with her. I felt like this was an intrusion into my privacy and grief and remember feeling angry at her. She wrote a letter that was handed to me the day before the funeral, saying why she hadn't come alone, and how she felt, and thanking me for always being there for her in the past – but then ended with saying she wouldn't be there for me at the funeral as she couldn't face it; she was scared. The rage boiled inside me. Maybe I should have understood it was difficult for others too, but instead I felt betrayed, let down and disappointed. How could she not want to be there, to be beside me when I needed her to be, to be with me in this, my darkest hour? Maybe everyone felt like that; maybe I would end up truly alone, like someone with a most contagious disease sentenced to indefinite quarantine. Is this how it would be? I had lost my child, my first born, my beautiful little girl, and for that I was being punished and made to spend a life in absolute solitude? Suddenly instead of anger I felt an unrelenting fear, her words echoing around the room. I read them over and over but each time the reality of what life would now possibly be like for a mother who had lost her child seemed ever more daunting. My life had changed forever; I would no longer be Debbie –

people would refer to me as the 'girl whose baby died', possibly stare at me, maybe even cross the road to avoid me for fear of not knowing what to say, just like my friend was avoiding me because she couldn't deal with it. She was scared! I was numb.

The evening before the funeral I couldn't sleep; I sat downstairs all night, still, my whole body weak, my head feeling like it was in a vice and the tears just flowing like a trickle from a leaky tap that couldn't be fixed. How can a parent bury their child, I kept asking myself; it just isn't the way life is meant to work out.

That morning flowers started arriving early and were placed on the front lawn. I couldn't bring myself to look. Eventually it began to look like a flower bed in full bloom, but I couldn't read the cards; I had no idea where they were coming from – friends, family and neighbours I suspected. I did wonder whether her dad had sent anything, or even his parents, but I left the thoughts to linger. I didn't want to go outside; I was scared I may lose my temper and destroy all the floral tributes. I could envisage flower heads flying through the air and landing like snowflakes of all colours all over the grass verges outside; stay put, I told myself, it's not their fault, they are just sending flowers because your little girl is gone. GONE. I fell to my knees; I didn't know if I had the strength to stand, let alone walk, and yet I had to. I had to lay my little angel to rest.

Neighbours began to gather outside the house and

I was awash with utter dread. I knew I would see the stares, the whispering, the look of pity on their faces. I was struggling to put one foot in front of the other. The funeral cars began to arrive and Terry came into the house, asking, "Are you ready?" I wanted to scream, "Of course I'm not ready, who an earth could ever would be ready for this?" I couldn't speak. My mom took my arm and helped me out of the house. My little sister and brother would be staying home with a family friend; they were too young to experience the grief of a child's funeral. They had been thrown into a tornado of disruption they didn't understand; they couldn't comprehend at their age what was happening – it was best they stayed home. My other sister and brother who were much older would be with me in the family car with my parents.

The flowers were beginning to disappear as they were loaded into the funeral car. I was shocked by the size of the casket, and I held my breath. I wanted to run up and grab it and run away with my baby girl. I began to sob uncontrollably, totally unaware of all the onlookers and who was next to me. I know I made it to the car and church, but for that moment in time it was all once again a blur. I came back to earth once the cars stopped outside the church doors.

I immediately noticed his parents standing there; they appeared awkward and stood off to the side from all the others waiting to enter the church. I looked around, my eyes searching – was he there, did he come? I couldn't see him; maybe he was hiding out of sight, feeling ashamed? I would find out soon enough, I thought; it's hard to hide in the small church.

The tiny casket was withdrawn from the hearse and my dad stepped forward. I had asked that he carry my little girl. It must have been traumatic for my dad too, having to hold his granddaughter, his first grandchild not in his arms but in a tiny white casket. He lifted the tiny casket and began walking towards the church aisle. I was holding on to my mom like my life depended upon it, as if once again I could see that big black hole opening up. I couldn't let go. We began to walk behind my dad and my daughter, the weight of each step seeming to become heavier and more difficult. The casket was placed on a tiny table at the front of the church, and everyone took their seats.

The whole ceremony seemed to proceed without my hearing a word that was being said by the vicar. It was as though I was in a some sort of a coma; I could hear sounds and voices but couldn't make out any of the words. My vision was blurred; was I even there? Was I awake? Was this all really just a bad nightmare? If only...

Once the service ended, the vicar advised the congregation that the burial would immediately follow the service, and to proceed behind the funeral cars to Jade's resting place. The cemetery was only a short drive away, no more than 15 minutes. As we left the church and returned to the waiting funeral car I looked around, searching the mourners. He wasn't there; he hadn't even made it to her funeral. What kind of father was he or would he have been?

The burial plot was a double and I knew that I would be with her again one day, the way I felt I wanted to be there with her now. My life felt as though I was in a dark cold place; I couldn't see any light, just deep emptiness. Why was I here? I should be with my Jade.

The cars arrived at the cemetery and we were directed to the plot. I felt like the skies were falling in on me; again my breathing began to race, my chest tightened and the tears flowed like a never ending stream. Everything was surreal; it was as if it were an out of body experience. I could hear the sobbing and anguish – it was deafening – and then I realised it was my own sobbing I could hear.

My baby was being laid to rest. The casket was lowered and I stumbled. I wanted to jump in after her; I couldn't leave her there, how could I, what kind of a mom would do that? My family were each holding a white rose, all waiting for me to go first with the earth and rose. I gripped the rose so tightly I cut my hand on one of the thorns, and when I was handed some earth I must have swapped the rose to my other hand because I remember the sting of the earth in the open cut on my palm. I just stood there for what seemed like ages. Eventually Terry came to me; he held my arm between my wrist and elbow and guided me towards the edge of the dug hole, encouraging me to let go of the earth. I don't recall even doing it, but I must have as my family followed and then the roses were let to flow too. I held onto my rose and went last, as if in doing so I would be delaying my goodbye. My feet seemed as though they were permanently fixed in place, blocks of cement securing them where my baby would be. I couldn't move. The funeral goers began to come over to me before leaving – my mom glued to my side had never moved – and as each person left, the area became serene and yet still it all felt surreal. It was then that I realised his parents hadn't been to the interment. I felt devastated; her father had been a complete no show and her grandparents had shown a half-hearted attempt. How could either of them be so cruel and unemotional? His first born, their first grandchild, and yet it seemed a burden not a loss to them. It was incomprehensible; even in my state of feeling numb I still couldn't comprehend their callousness.

From that moment on the rest of the day was unremarkable and not something I wished to remember. I recall going back to my parents' house, but how we got there and when we left the cemetery I do not know. I went straight to my room; I couldn't face any more of the day. With hindsight, leaving my mom to deal with it was selfish, but I couldn't think of anything or anyone but my little star, my Jade. I could see her face so vividly in my mind, forever engraved in my memory.

Being laid to rest is being at peace, they say. I wanted peace; I wanted to be with her, to hold her, to tell her how much I loved her. Whatever it took, I was sure I was going to be with her ... soon.

CHAPTER 6

Picking up the pieces

The days that followed her funeral didn't bring peace or closure. I couldn't accept she was gone. Had I failed her? What had I done wrong? What if I hadn't gone to the Isle of Man; had it been too much strain on the pregnancy? Had I been so upset and angry that I could have caused my little girl to gain her wings too soon? Why hadn't her dad been in touch? Was he even back in the UK? Was he still living with his so-called convenient girlfriend? Did he even care about his daughter, let alone me and what I was going through alone?

So many questions were going through my mind.

Why hadn't the hospital known she wasn't growing?

Why hadn't they scanned me when they were supposed to?

Would she have survived if she had been delivered and in the neo-natal ward as they thought she would be?

I lived in hope that I would get some answers at my next appointment, and maybe the answers would help to ease the pain and frustrations that besieged my mind and body every minute, hour and day, and plagued my sleep every night.

Since coming home from the hospital and at the funeral I had been handed many cards and received many letters, yet all but a few remained unopened. One day I felt it was time to read the words of others, and each card I opened wrenched my stomach. I had letters from Hazel's mother in Daventry, one from Dawn in the Isle of Man, and another from Eileen the midwife, with a beautiful tiny sterling silver St Christopher, which she sent as a keepsake in memory of my little angel.

Aside from the funeral, I hadn't left the house since coming home from the hospital. The funeral experience itself was harrowing enough, but my mom and Lesley insisted almost daily that I needed to venture out. They said I needed fresh air – like the air outside was going to cure me somehow – and that I needed to try to gain some normality. 'Normality!' I could hear myself screaming in my head. Nothing will ever be normal again, you people are insane and insensitive! How could I ever feel any kind of normal again? A piece of me and my whole being had been cruelly snatched away, taken without my consent, without notice, without consideration. Whatever version of normal they envisaged for me, it would never be 'normal' to me again.

It was by now almost December; the tradition in our house had always been to put the tree up on 1 December every year. Christmas had always been my favourite time of the year; growing up with four siblings meant it was always bedlam, chaotic and fun. We were always having family and friends around over the festive period, the games and drinks were endless and the fun lasted from before Christmas until after my birthday on New Year's Eve, sometimes even days after New Year. But this year, this year I was filled with dread. It should have been a happy, joyous time, married to my first love and enjoying our first Christmas with our daughter – I should have been a wife and mother. Instead I was alone. Neither would be with me. How could I even think of joyous times when all I wanted to do was be with my little girl. Seriously? Normal? What was anyone thinking when they suggested getting back to normal?

I continued writing poems for Jade, and as always the words just seemed to write themselves.

> *It's been three weeks yet still it seems*
> *I'll never mend these broken dreams*
> *To hold you once just wasn't enough*
> *For your baby face I long to touch*
> *You came to me from up above*
> *My own little girl to cherish and love*
> *But God decided my heart he'd break*

BORN AN ANGEL

For from my arms, a little angel he'd take
Though in my thoughts you will always stay
My love for you will grow each passing day

**

I sit alone now and silently cry
I never thought we'd say goodbye
Some things are just not meant forever
I always thought we'd be together
Sometimes the pain's too much to bear
The memories we will never share
What once was two is now just one
I still can't believe that you are gone
I look for you now and know you're not there
I would search for you but I don't know where
For you're now gone, how is this true
A stranger I am now, I left with you
If I could find some possible way
The price I'd pay for you to stay
But it cannot be, we can't go back
Now I walk alone a lonely path

**

The day that you were taken
My heart did split in two
One half filled with pain

The other left with you
Now I lay awake at night
When all the world's asleep
I think of you and of the day
We once again shall meet

**

After much insistence and coercion I finally succumbed to the requests to leave the house, and agreed to a walk to the local shops with my mom. I couldn't face going alone, but I agreed I would go under the safety of being with my mom.

As I got ready I could feel the anxiety levels rising; I felt as though someone was crushing my chest and my breathing began more laboured, so much so that it took several cups of tea and much more tenderness from my mom than I think either of us had ever anticipated, to just put on some shoes.

Eventually I was out the front door and making my way down the path. We walked slowly, and I gripped my mom's arm as hard as I could without cutting off her blood supply. Mom was patient and never lost her temper; she was gentle and understanding, and gave me words of comfort and reassurance each time my step faltered.

The walk should have taken five minutes, ten at the most, but it took nearly half an hour and many attempts to turn back, trying to convince Mom I couldn't do it. Each time she would encourage me to take another step, and finally we did reach the shops.

At first no one seemed to notice me, and I thought to myself, 'This isn't so bad, I can do this.' Then I began to notice things. First two young girls I recognised from school; they looked over, I could see them say something to each other and they looked again before they carried on walking, not even acknowledging me. I thought maybe I was being paranoid, maybe it was a self-fulfilling prophecy; of course people would talk, but they would talk *to* you too, wouldn't they? How very wrong was I. Even people who had known my parents for some considerable time, who had lived on the estate more than 20 years and worked locally, just seemed to half smile towards us and then head off in a different direction. I knew I wasn't imagining it; I knew this would happen. No longer was I 'Debbie from school', or 'the girl who was on TV'. Now I had the title of 'the one who's baby just died'. I cannot imagine how my parents had been dealing with this each time they had encountered people; how had they felt when people spoke to them or maybe even avoided them too. I needed to go home. Mom hadn't even finished her shopping, but I was becoming frantic – I needed to go back to the safety of my home NOW. Mom reluctantly agreed and said she would return to finish getting what she needed later, and we turned for home. I had no problems walking now, and my feet were moving at a pace that the rest of my body seemed to have difficulty keeping up with. On the way back I noticed one of our neighbours on the other side of the road, and I recall that what stuck in my mind is that they never crossed over to our side even though their house was this side. They appeared to wait until we had reached our front gate before starting to cross the road to theirs. Was this how it was going to be from now on, forever feeling alone and isolated? Hadn't I suffered enough? Hadn't my mom?

That was it, I thought, I would never leave the house again. People who had known my family and me for years wouldn't or couldn't speak to even say 'hello' anymore. It seemed I had become something of a leper carrying some awful contagious disease no one wanted to catch; I was unapproachable. I wanted to scream at them, 'Say something!' There was never going to be a right thing to say – how could there be – nothing said could change what had happened. I knew that, but wanted people to say something even if was the wrong thing. I felt as though I was being punished further; not only had my fiancé left and my daughter been taken from me, but now neighbours and friends avoided me. Would I ever live life again? Maybe I didn't deserve it, maybe it was all my fault, all of it.

Mid December, there had still been no word from Jade's dad. Each time the phone rang I waited, hoping it might be him, but it never was. The disappointment and rejection I felt only added to the pain, the grief and the hurt. I still hadn't written a single card or purchased any gifts for my family – so unlike me, I was normally fully prepared and well into the swing of the festive season, earning the nickname from my family of 'Mommy Christmas'. I loved giving, and Christmas shopping was the biggest thrill and enjoyment I got from each passing year, but not this year. Maybe never again. How would I explain to my little brother and sister why Father Christmas hadn't brought them a present from me this year? They already looked at me with trepidation each morning, not knowing whether to speak to me, whether I would answer or break down and cry. They were too young to understand. My other brother and sister understood only too well being much older; they had both tried to act as normal as possible around me, but more often than not conversations were short if at all existent. I think my eldest brother was grateful for being able to go back to his own home and not have to live with it 24 hours a day, seven days a week like my other siblings and parents. A few friends had been to visit occasionally and tried to convince me to go back to our local pub with them where previously we had met several times a week, but I hadn't felt up to it. The trip to the shops had set me back quite a bit, and being enclosed in a space with people staring and whispering, or so I thought they might, was not something I wanted to experience.

Eventually I went shopping for some presents, with my mom by my side yet again, at another local high street; a place where I wouldn't know everyone and could keep my head down and pretend for a day I was normal. I got through it, and when I returned home Mom was so proud of me. Although the heavy feeling in my stomach remained, I did feel a sense of achievement – I thought I wouldn't be able to do it, but I did. I knew nothing would ever be the same; I missed my daughter every waking second, and even in my sporadic periods of sleep I would wake and remember that she wasn't there, and then the visions and memories of that day would flood back into my mind again – the white walls, the doctor at the end of my bed, the surreal feeling that it was happening to someone else and not me. Maybe time would heal, but the scar was still very deep and very much on show; it wasn't easy to hide, and I didn't know if I ever could or would want to hide it away.

In a few days I was due back at the hospital. I was hoping with eager anticipation that I would get some answers and some closure, but I knew that going back there would be hard. The last time I had been there I had left my baby girl behind. I had never wanted to return there, but I needed answers.

The next few days waiting for the appointment seemed to drag endlessly. I watched the time pass slowly by, each minute feeling like an hour, each hour like a day, and when the morning of 19 December finally arrived Mom and I were ready early. I had a copy of my letter with me and felt both nervous and eager at the same time. Would I finally get some closure? Would I get the explanation I sought? Would there be a reason? Was I to blame? Were the doctors or hospital staff to blame? Or was it just God's way and there would be no explanation, no closure? Was my little girl destined to be born an angel from the very point of conception? Once again my head swam with questions and scenarios.

I sat at the dining table. Our kitchen ran the length of the house, and the dining table was near the entrance door at the front of the house; a teak veneer table with six chairs. A further dining set was at the back of the lounge – after all there were so many of us, seating was a need not a decoration – and the kitchen cupboards and appliances sat to the rear of the house, with the sink at the far end looking out over the back garden. Mom stood near the sink making a cup of tea. She looked at me with an expression of anguish; like me, she too must have been filled with dread that we would have no definitive answers, that we would come back still filled with questions and that I would never find closure and be able to accept my loss or the hand that fate had dealt me. My only hope was that someday I could learn to live with the tragedy, emptiness and loss, because if I couldn't there would be no more options for me. I had fought daily with the feelings and yearning to be with my little girl for the past several weeks, existing and not living, holding on to the only thing that kept me going – my mom. How could I put her through what I was enduring? Hadn't she too suffered enough? She didn't need to say anything; Mom and I had developed this sixth sense between us since Jade had left us. It was a mother–daughter bond that not only was I grateful for and had become undeniably dependent upon, but one that we both knew was unique and unconditional; she had been my rock, my confidante, my verbal punching bag – undeservedly on occasion – and yet she took it all and still loved me without bounds, despite all the heartache she herself was suffering. No mother should have to deal with the loss of a child, and likewise no mother should have to watch her child deal with such a loss either. I would forever be in her debt for all she had offered, sustained and persevered with during the past several weeks, and possibly for longer still, although she would have said, 'you owe me nothing, I am your mother,' with nothing but hope in her eyes and love in her heart.

Finally the time came to leave. Lesley had offered to take us and arrived promptly. The journey wasn't long, and we were soon outside the hospital once again; the memories flooded into my mind inducing a raging tornado of emotions. I felt the urge to scream and run, but mom grabbed my hand as if she had read my mind. We weren't going anywhere but inside to get answers, of this she was certain. I wished at that moment that I could have had even an ounce of the same strength and determination that she did; she had been remarkable throughout all of this.

We sat in the magnolia painted waiting room on the plastic blue, extremely uncomfortable, chairs, the smell undeniable and a further reminder of where I was and why I was here. The last time I had been in this waiting room I had been several months' pregnant with no indication of what lay ahead. In fact, just before my appointment, I had visited a clairvoyant along with a friend. The clairvoyant had told me he could see tears, but he said they were tears of joy. I had never really believed fully in psychics, but I did wonder now whether he had known what lay in wait for me, and rather than tell me had added the words 'of joy' to the end of his sentence.

Mr Crawford himself called us into the office, no understudy this time. On previous appointments he hadn't always been in attendance, but not this time. I had the attention of the man himself. He wore a pale grey shirt and his blue tie loose around his collar; he looked at me with pity and sorrow in his eyes as everyone before him had. We sat down and he began firstly by saying how sorry he was for my loss and that he had received my letter and a copy had been passed to the board. I felt the tears welling up in my eyes, and then he began to speak about each point in turn. It soon became apparent that there were some serious flaws in my care and that they hadn't as yet been able to ascertain the full extent of and explanation for this, but the final summary was that the pre-eclampsia had resulted in distress to Jade, who was already distressed following the haemorrhaging at 29 weeks. She hadn't in fact grown much at all since that time, and despite this being on the notes, no one had thought that bringing her out early would have changed the outcome. I disagreed, and left with bulging eyes and a sinking heart, feeling that all I had been told was that they had decided that she didn't have a chance at survival so they had just been waiting for the inevitable.

I was filled now with fury and anger. How could they decide to play God with my baby's life, how dare they! I went home with Mom thinking about the next stages. Lesley had already informed me that many processes had been changed and new ones implemented at the hospital following my letter, and a review of the procedures was in place. I told her how I felt and asked whether I should seek further advice. She said, 'You have to do what you have to do, but ask yourself, will anything bring Jade back? Will it ease your suffering or prolong it?' I didn't have the answers. My mom looked at me once again anguished, dreading what we would all go through if I pursued this. I decided that despite my sense of rage I couldn't put my mom through anymore; but how could I live with this, accepting that I would never know if Jade had been given a fair chance at life and I at being her mom?

The next few days were fraught with mixed emotions. The younger siblings were becoming increasingly excited and I was trying with every ounce of energy I had to smile for them, to not bring the festive feelings crashing to the ground, but everything looked wrong. The bright lights, glistening decorations, wrapped gifts all around the base of the tree, the cupboards that were beginning to bulge with the once a year Christmas food treats, tubs of chocolates still unopened near the tree – we were never allowed to open them until after Christmas dinner when we all sat down to watch a family film – and the flurry of visitors bringing cards and gifts. All quite normal, but not for me, not this year, nor ever again.

CHAPTER 7

A new start

On Christmas Eve 1990, not at all feeling the Christmas spirit, I put on a brave face for my family. My mom urged me to try to be a little upbeat for the sake of my younger sister and brother, who were annoyingly excited and were no way intending on getting any sleep that evening. They were convinced they could stay awake all night and catch Father Christmas bringing their presents, despite being told he won't come if you stay awake. It was the same tradition every year; ever since we were little we would leave out a glass of whisky and a mince pie for Father Christmas, and a carrot and a glass of milk for Rudolph. I'm pretty sure Dad got the Father Christmas tot and pie, while mom dealt with Rudolph's milk and cut up the carrot to add to the already prepared vegetables in the saucepan of water on the stove, leaving just the nobble on the plate. Dad had orders to leave crumbs on the plate from the mince pie but he certainly never left any whisky in the glass.

The morning of Christmas Day no one was allowed to come downstairs until Mom had been into the kitchen to make a pot of tea. She had always prepared all the cups on a tray the night before, as well as the potatoes and vegetables for dinner; the turkey would have been put in the oven over night to cook slowly, and the smell would reach upstairs all through the night. Early morning we would all sit at the top of the stairs waiting for mom and dad to go into the lounge to check if Father Christmas had been, and then fight one another to get down the stairs first. How there was never any serious accidents is an absolute miracle with all the pushing and shoving. The lounge would look like a scene from Santa's grotto; five huge Christmas sacks always brimming over with gifts, a huge lit Christmas tree, and my parents' presents were always left under the tree with the tubs of chocolates. They would open theirs last once all ours were open; how they ever found them under the mountains of ripped wrapping paper was yet another miracle, but after all, wasn't Christmas the time for miracles? Christmas at our house, come rain or shine, pounds or pennies, my parents had always managed to give us the best Christmases, always ones to remember. I knew this one would be one to remember for me and not how all the others had been remembered before. I knew I would look back on this Christmas with a hollow heart and not one full of the love and joy of Christmases gone by.

Nonetheless, I had faithfully promised my ever loving mother I would give it my best shot, and I owed her that at least. Christmas Eve was a busy day in our house; lots of comings and goings, the little ones running riot, dressed in their pyjamas by 4pm thinking it would make the next day come quicker, food preparations going on, table decorations being brought out from the loft, last minute gifts to wrap and, of course, checking there was enough of the merry juice to go around should any extra visitors drop by.

I busied myself most of the day, trying to push the emptiness I still felt in my stomach to the back of my mind, reminding myself I owed it to my family after all they had done for me, trying not to spoil Christmas.

My friends had been asking for the past few days if I would join them at the local just for a short while. No one other than a few close friends had seen me since I had been admitted to hospital back in October. Initially I was adamant I would not go, but as the day progressed and the chaos occupied my thoughts more I began to anticipate maybe going just for a short while – I mean, it couldn't really hurt, could it? I would be with people I knew and who knew me and what had happened, and anyone else there probably wouldn't have a clue and would be too preoccupied with the festivities to give me a second glance. So maybe I would go, maybe it would turn out to be a nice evening.

By 6pm I had decided I would go and began getting ready. My mom was overjoyed that I had decided to go out, although concerned about my potential reaction and how I would handle the busy pub. She said that if at any time I became overwhelmed and felt I needed to come home, to call her and get a taxi – she would pay once I got back. Normally I would walk or get the bus, but one of my girlfriends suggested picking me up. We would drive back to hers and leave the car there, then walk to the pub. It was only a short walk from where she lived and I didn't want to walk into the pub alone anyway, so the proposal worked for me. She arrived about 7pm and I was dressed and had applied some make up. I had bought a new cream blouse with very puffed up shoulders and large gold buttons that I put on with a black skirt and long boots. By now I had lost so much weight that nothing I owned fitted me properly, so a new outfit was much needed. Although I still felt far from ready emotionally, I headed out the door promising my mom I would be back at a reasonable time and would not wake the little siblings – not that I imagined for one moment they would be properly asleep in any case, or that I would be out long.

My girlfriend, like my mother, glowed with excitement that I had finally agreed to go out. She promised faithfully to stay with me and make sure I was OK. We left the car as arranged outside her house and walked to the pub; it was a dry, crisp evening, the houses were all lit up and Christmas trees could be seen glowing in all the windows with open curtains. The streets were littered with people coming and going from houses, either visiting friends and relatives or making their way to and from local establishments. There was an air of happiness and peacefulness all around, and for the first time in several weeks I felt a little more at ease. Something I never imagined I would ever feel again since Bonfire Night, since my little girl became a bright shining star. That thought made me look straight to the skies above; my eyes searched and there she was – I could see her shining bright, so bright my eyes hurt to stare at her. I had stopped walking to look up and my friend was looking to me and then the sky wondering what I was doing. I explained, and she put her arms around me and gave me a huge hug, and said, 'She will always be with you, watching over you, she's your guardian angel now.'

We finally reached the local public house, a place I had frequented many evenings before becoming poorly during my pregnancy. It had been almost six months since I had been through the doors, and it was a strange feeling walking towards them now, knowing life was so different to how it had been the last time I was here. I wasn't sure what the reception inside would be, neither did I have any notion of how I might react once inside, but when I entered our friends spotted us immediately.

They were all congregated to the right of the entrance and crowded around two tables; everyone in turn came over to me and expressed both their regret for little Jade and in turn their joy that I had decided to make an appearance. One said it was her Christmas wish that I would finally come and be with them all again. There were around 20 of us in total, and they seemed to cocoon me all night, as if knowing I didn't want the attention of others. I felt safe, and for the first time since losing Jade I felt something return inside me; not filling the void, but taking a little edge away.

One of the lads in the group, Joshua, whom I hadn't previously seen eye to eye with, had apparently put the most into the collection for the flowers for Jade, I was told that evening. This took me aback somewhat, as we hadn't exactly exchanged pleasantries before and the negative feelings had been mutual, so I was very touched by the gesture. Later that evening he came over to speak with me, and I expressed my thanks for his generosity; but now something was different between us – it seemed as though we suddenly had a connection that had never been there before. Maybe just a genuine understanding, but a mutual respect was definitely there for the first time in the three years we had known one another. We chatted frequently throughout the night on and off. I chatted with almost everyone, and once the initial, 'how are you, so sorry' sentences were out of the way everyone managed to act normal, and I felt myself actually beginning to enjoy the evening. At one point I went to the bathroom, excusing myself – I felt so guilty being there, for not being home – I should be home mourning my little girl, I kept thinking, but at the same time it was as if something was urging me to re-join my friends. I succumbed to the latter feeling and went back to the group.

The evening was finally coming to a close. It was well after 11pm and I had promised I would be home no later than midnight. I decided I would walk, as getting a taxi would be hell and a long wait. One of the guys in the group, who I knew had always liked me, offered to walk me home. He was very drunk himself, and even if I was interested in a relationship he unfortunately wasn't my type – he was too nice, I suppose you would say, and drank way too much and too often. Seeing my discomfort at trying to dissuade him from walking, well, stumbling, home with me, Joshua came over and told him that he had already agreed to walk me home and suggested we start walking. With that we said our good nights and set off. Despite Joshua living close to the pub he said he was happy to walk me home and then walk back.

Surprisingly we chatted all the way home and it turned out we actually had a lot in common. Three years and we had never spoken; it turned out we each had a preconception of the other and hadn't actually taken the time, for whatever reason, to get to know one another. In fairness we had both had partners, both of whom were the jealous type, and so our talking before may have caused issues, but now we were both single and having a wonderful chat during the walk home. It was actually after midnight when we finally reached my house. We wished each other a happy Christmas and exchanged a little kiss before he turned to walk back home, agreeing to see one another again on Boxing Day. Before I went indoors I looked up to the sky and I swear that my little star was winking at me. I felt a certain aura of peacefulness pass over me and I'm sure something or someone touched my face and stroked my cheek, but no one was there. I must have imagined it – or did I? Was my guardian angel nearby?

CHAPTER 8

My family

Joshua and I had been together ever since that Christmas Eve. Neither of us had been looking for a relationship, but things progressed naturally as if with no thought or effort at all, despite having all the odds stacked against us. No one ever imagined for one moment that we were at all compatible and would last the course; many of his friends even told him in the early days that he should stay clear as I was only after another baby. Really? Did they honestly think I would be looking to replace my daughter? Nothing and no one could do that; she was my first born, my shining star, my forever love, no replacement needed nor possible.

By the Christmas of 1992, however, we did touch on the subject of children, and by March 1993 we were announcing our pregnancy. Joshua, unlike Jade's dad, had a steady job and a car – a metallic blue XR3i Cabriolet with a black canvas soft roof. He was so proud of that car and washed it every single week. I had passed my test and got my first car, a white Ford Escort, just six weeks before and had a steady job in the city centre – I had been working there almost two years as an accounts administrator.

We broke the news to our parents and both were over the moon – a totally different reception to the announcement of my pregnancy with Jade.

Obviously I was going to be monitored extremely closely. My younger sister had given birth the previous year to her first child, a little boy, and now I would be adding once again to the already large family. Christmases were going to get even more chaotic, it seemed, with a new generation emerging.

I decided I would return to the same hospital, my thought process being that all I had were bad memories – maybe I could make some happier ones there. As they knew my history and were unlikely to want any repeat, I believed my care would be exceptional this time. I knew it wouldn't be easy, and it would probably be emotionally straining to go back there, but I felt it was something I needed to do.

My previous consultant was no longer there, for which I was grateful as I would have refused his care. My new consultant was a large, softly spoken man with a cheery face, and he assured me from our first meeting that there was no possibility of anything being missed or overlooked, not on his watch.

The pregnancy went smoothly. I gained an excessive amount of weight, mostly because I wasn't allowed to do anything; everyone rallied around me making sure I didn't overdo anything or get stressed or upset – in fact I was very spoilt.

I had never heard from Jade's dad, not once since I had left the Isle of Man, although I understood he had returned home. Not that I was in any way interested – I had a new life and a new start and it didn't include him – but it would always include Jade, she would never be forgotten.

On Monday 27 September a meal was arranged; both my parents and Joshua's were invited. My due date was a few weeks off. I had been given a date of 18 October and it was fast approaching. I was by now on maternity leave from my job and was like a beached whale, but I didn't care; as long as my baby was growing I didn't care how big I got. My thought process was that the extra padding was keeping my baby safe. We didn't know what we were expecting; gender scans still weren't available unless you paid privately, which wasn't an option for us as we were in the process of buying our first home and all available funds were going into creating a home for our new arrival. Joshua had even sold the XR3i to be able to buy a new kitchen and he was now using my car, my little Escort, but we didn't care; we were happy.

Unfortunately his parents couldn't make the meal, which was a shame as it was the last time we would be together as parents to be; that Friday, 1 October, my waters broke in the early hours of the morning, and I went straight to the hospital.

I was taken to the labour ward and after an examination was advised that only my front waters had ruptured and the back were still intact. The midwife on duty wanted to send me back home until the back waters ruptured, but my mom and Joshua were with me and Mom very sternly pointed out that the previous errors made meant we would not leave until we had seen my consultant. He arrived on the labour ward shortly afterwards, and as promised he said I was going nowhere and that the baby was being born that day. He arranged for my back waters to be ruptured; I was hooked up to the baby monitor and baby's heart beat was strong. It was then that Joshua pulled a ring box from his pocket. He looked at me with the ring box open, and I accepted without hesitation. Was this really happening? Had I been given a second shot at happiness? Had my little Jade swapped her life for her wings so that I may have a chance of having the 'fairy tale', the 'happy ever after' I had dreamed of when I had first met Jade's father? I was overwhelmed with feelings of joy. Joshua placed the ring on my finger, and it was a perfect fit; his uncle was a diamond setter and had made the ring himself – a unique ring just for me. It had a single, large diamond set in the centre of what looked like a swirl of gold; it was beautiful. Apparently the meal on the Monday had been arranged so that he could propose in front of our parents – both sets of parents were aware, but unfortunate events had meant his parents could not make it – and he had rearranged for that weekend, not expecting our bundle of joy to ruin the moment by deciding to arrive early. Everything was perfect, a far cry from three years previously.

But then suddenly things went drastically wrong. As soon as my back waters ruptured, the baby's heart beat become erratic and big drops on the print out were evident. My consultant wasted no time, and within minutes I was being unhooked and pushed towards the theatre, Joshua was sent to get a theatre gown on, and I was under anaesthetic before I could even think about possible outcomes.

When I finally woke, Joshua was sat on the bed next to me, eyes red and bulging from crying. I was still groggy, and I didn't know what had happened. Dear God, what was going on? Why was he crying? Where was my baby? Please let my baby be OK. Joshua kissed my forehead and then moved aside slightly – and there she was: in an incubator, but alive, rosy cheeks, a mass of dark brown hair, so tiny. I cried too. I couldn't hold her just yet; we were both wired up to so many machines, there were wires coming from everywhere, but I didn't care; I knew I would hold her soon and forever. I knew the most precious thing I would ever have around my neck from this day forward were the arms of my little girl.

Apparently it had been touch and go for a while. The baby's heartbeat had dropped to almost nothing, and Joshua hadn't even had chance to get changed before the surgeons had brought her into the world. She was here before he had finished doing up his theatre gown. He had broken down – he thought he had lost us both – but we came through, and now we would be complete. Engaged to be married and a proper little family unit.

My consultant had kept his word and made sure this time my little girl was properly taken care of and safely brought into this world. It was going to be a long recovery following the emergency caesarean section, but I didn't care. The pain would be physical not emotional this time, and I had come through worse, much worse. Just looking at her tiny nose and fingers made everything that had and was to come worthwhile.

I would tell her when she was older about her big sister. Jade would never be forgotten; she was born an angel and will forever be by my side. The saying goes that things happen for a reason, but that reason is not always readily evident. For three years I felt I had no reasoning or explanation for Jade; now I wondered if maybe this was it – that my little angel knew the life I would, she would, have endured had she have survived would be a lonely existence, her father not wanting to know either of us, struggling to make ends meet. Did she somehow know, did she want better for both of us, is that why she gained her wings so soon? I told myself that my beautiful angel had given her life selflessly so that I may have a happy, safe, loving life and family. She would forever be my guardian angel, my daughter, my first born, and I would make sure she was never ever forgotten.

Just weeks before my daughter was born, Shelley gave birth to a little girl too. The items that had been stored in the attic by her parents when tragedy had struck us both had now been retrieved, washed, and were in full use.

Shelley and I continued to play a big part in each other's lives. This time the outcome had been different for both of us, and ironically our timing seemed synchronised again, but this time we were both holding our daughters filled with different tears, tears of joy. We both understood that our little girls could never be replaced, but we had a second chance and we were going to take that chance with both hands and relish every second. When you have lost something so precious, someone you loved before you had even met them, someone who has touched your life in a way you can and will never forget, then the next chance you get seems even more profound, because you understand how lucky you are to have that chance to hold, love, protect, care for and cherish every precious moment.

CHAPTER 9

Author's note

Two years later, following another emergency Caesarean section, another baby daughter joined our family and we felt we were then complete. This time Shelley and I weren't in sync; it was some five years later that Shelley gave birth to another baby girl.

Over time I learned not to show the scars of losing Jade too often, but when people used to ask how many children I had I would say three. I knew that if they asked more questions I would tell them about Jade, and I was aware it made them uncomfortable – in fact it killed the conversation and once again the person would soon distance themselves. Eventually I began to stop saying I had three daughters and would say two, just to save anyone the discomfort that clearly showed.

I found it difficult to comprehend and I was filled with an overwhelming sense of guilt; it was as if I were hiding a dirty secret and not a tragic loss. I went through some very low stages. I had two beautiful daughters running around, but I always had three daughters with me.

It took a lot of time to be brave enough to go back to answering the question 'how many children do you have?' with 'I have three daughters'. I was prepared to suffer the isolation in social events that I knew my reply may bring; she is my daughter, my first born and I intend to ensure I keep her memory well and truly alive and not hide her to save the feelings of others – because then who considers my feelings? Who will continue to ensure Jade's memory is kept alive?

Even now people I know and love, and who know about my little angel, often suggest that I don't mention my daughter and my loss, but I won't succumb to such a request. I will not feel guilt or anguish or hide the memory of my daughter in order to spare others, mostly strangers, and to ease their discomfort. I have lived through one of life's most tragic moments, the loss of a child. It is not something to be hidden, to feel guilty about; it is reality, it is life and it still happens today. No one is immune, regardless of stature or wealth, and maybe if the subject was not so taboo, and if those of us who suffer the loss can talk openly without feeling as if we are being alienated, then maybe we can heal quicker, and the memories and legacies of the angels who got their wings too soon – at whatever age and for whatever reason, if there is one – can be kept alive as they should be.

*****

The Still Birth and Neonatal Death Society (Sands), who this year are celebrating their 40th anniversary, have kindly given their permission for being referenced in this book, and have provided the following statement:

'The views expressed in this book are not necessarily the views of Sands'.

Sands exists to support anyone affected by the death of a baby, to improve the bereavement care received by parents and families and to influence policy makers and promote research to reduce the number of babies dying. Sands' Freephone helpline number is 0808 164 3332, and their email address is: helpline@sands.org.uk